Editor-in-Chief and Founder:
  Lyndon H. LaRouche, Jr.
Editorial Board: *Lyndon H. LaRouche, Jr. , Helga
  Zepp-LaRouche, Robert Ingraham, Tony
  Papert, Gerald Rose, Dennis Small, Jeffrey
  Steinberg, William Wertz*
Co-Editors: *Robert Ingraham, Tony Papert*
Technology: *Marsha Freeman*
Books: *Katherine Notley*
Ebooks: *Richard Burden*
Graphics: *Alan Yue*
Photos: *Stuart Lewis*
Circulation Manager: *Stanley Ezrol*

INTELLIGENCE DIRECTORS
Counterintelligence: *Jeffrey Steinberg, Michele
  Steinberg*
Economics: *John Hoefle, Marcia Merry Baker,
  Paul Gallagher*
History: *Anton Chaitkin*
Ibero-America: *Dennis Small*
Russia and Eastern Europe: *Rachel Douglas*
United States: *Debra Freeman*

INTERNATIONAL BUREAUS
Bogotá: *Miriam Redondo*
Berlin: *Rainer Apel*
Copenhagen: *Tom Gillesberg*
Houston: *Harley Schlanger*
Lima: *Sara Madueño*
Melbourne: *Robert Barwick*
Mexico City: *Gerardo Castilleja Chávez*
New Delhi: *Ramtanu Maitra*
Paris: *Christine Bierre*
Stockholm: *Ulf Sandmark*
United Nations, N.Y.C.: *Leni Rubinstein*
Washington, D.C.: *William Jones*
Wiesbaden: *Göran Haglund*

ON THE WEB
e-mail: eirns@larouchepub.com
www.larouchepub.com
www.executiveintelligencereview.com
www.larouchepub.com/eiw
Webmaster: *John Sigerson*
Assistant Webmaster: *George Hollis*
Editor, Arabic-language edition: *Hussein Askary*

EIR (ISSN 0273-6314) *is published weekly
(50 issues), by EIR News Service, Inc.,
P.O. Box 17390, Washington, D.C. 20041-0390.
(703) 297-8434*

European Headquarters: E.I.R. GmbH, Postfach
Bahnstrasse 9a, D-65205, Wiesbaden, Germany
Tel: 49-611-73650
Homepage: http://www.eir.de
e-mail: info@eir.de
Director: Georg Neudecker

Montreal, Canada: 514-461-1557
eir@eircanada.ca

Denmark: EIR - Danmark, Sankt Knuds Vej 11,
basement left, DK-1903 Frederiksberg, Denmark.
Tel.: +45 35 43 60 40, Fax: +45 35 43 87 57. e-mail:
eirdk@hotmail.com.

Mexico City: EIR, Sor Juana Inés de la Cruz 242-2
Col. Agricultura C.P. 11360
Delegación M. Hidalgo, México D.F.
Tel. (5525) 5318-2301
eirmexico@gmail.com

Copyright: ©2017 EIR News Service. All rights
reserved. Reproduction in whole or in part without
permission strictly prohibited.

Canada Post Publication Sales Agreement
#40683579

Postmaster: Send all address changes to *EIR*, P.O.
Box 17390, Washington, D.C. 20041-0390.

Signed articles in *EIR* represent the views of the authors,
and not necessarily those of the Editorial Board.

Sputnik Shock

'LISTEN TO US NOW!'

Putin Delivers New Sputnik Shock

by Helga Zepp-LaRouche, Founder of the International Schiller Institutes

Mar. 2—In a trans-Atlantic atmosphere of hysteria against Russia and China that can only be understood as pre-war propaganda, President Putin dropped a bombshell in his annual State of the Union address, which has redefined the strategic balance. He announced that Russian forces had acquired weapons based on new physical principles, including a new intercontinental missile capable of travelling at 20 times the speed of sound, with excellent maneuverability. It can therefore outmaneuver all existing air defense and missile defense systems and render them obsolete. These new systems, he explained, which include nuclear-powered cruise missiles, fast drone submarines and laser weapons, were Russia's answer to the unilateral termination of the ABM Treaty by the U.S. in 2002, and the launch of the global U.S. missile defense system. Since then, all attempts at negotiation had fallen on deaf ears. "Nobody wanted to listen to us. So listen now!" Putin emphasized.

The response from the Western media and politicians ranged from attempts to ridicule Putin's new arsenals as technologically impossible, mere pre-election bluster, to concerns about a new arms race—as if it had not begun long ago, with NATO's eastward expansion.

Vladimir Putin delivers Presidential Address to the Federal Assembly, March 1.

kremlin.ru

These responses once again reflect the fact that adherents to neo-liberal dogma can only see the world through their geopolitical concave glasses, and they obviously underestimate Russia's military science capabilities, just as they underestimated the dynamics of China's New Silk Road for years.

Contrary to the opinion of the *Bild* newspaper, which compared Putin to a mouse squeaking at a lion, Putin is more likely to be the cat among the mice. With the creation of new varieties of weapons based on new physical principles, a level has been established which is very different from, for example, the fairly linear scenarios proposed by the recent CSIS think-tank report in which Russia and China are said to be preparing surprise attacks on the Baltic States or in the South China Sea. In other CSIS scenarios, it is mooted that China will attack the U.S. with cruise missiles to force it to withdraw from the Pacific, or that China would wipe out the entire American leadership in preparation for an invasion of Taiwan.

The reaction of the pro-party Chinese newspaper *Global Times*, in an article entitled "U.S. Frightened by its Own Mirror Image," put it in a nutshell: The U.S. has fallen into the trap that an expert at the Office of Net As-

Russian YU-74 hypersonic glide vehicle.

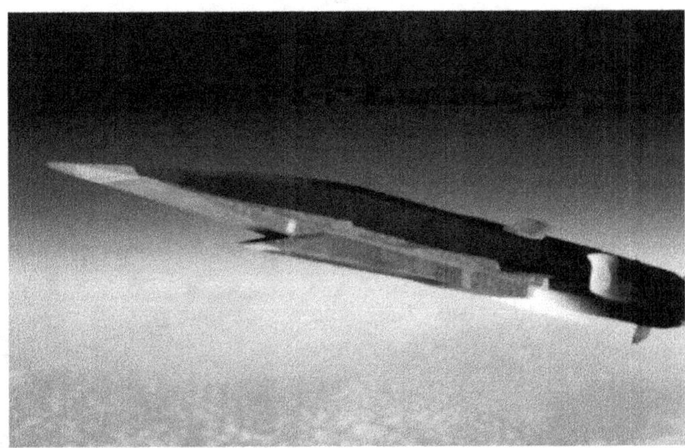

The YU-74 hypersonic glide missile will be carried atop a new ICBM, the RS-28.

sessment of the Pentagon had warned about. Andrew Marshall (who is otherwise responsible for a utopian doctrine of air war) had warned not to project one's own intentions onto the intentions of other states. For decades, the article notes, the U.S. has been pursuing a preventive-war military doctrine, while China's military doctrine aims to respond to an attack with a counterattack. Similarly, it is common American practice to eliminate hostile governments through regime change, while the Chinese Communist Party has rejected the idea of assassinating the leadership of hostile governments since the 1920s. And thirdly, it is U.S. policy to focus on nuclear arsenal development, even as a response to conventional threats and cyber-attacks, while China considers it unwise to own too many nuclear weapons, preferring instead to have only as many as are necessary for deterrence. Drawing conclusions from such mirror images has nothing to do with the real world, and if the U.S. military were to follow this study, the article concludes, they would be scared to death by their own shadow and fail to prepare for real dangers.

A knowledgeable analyst writing under the pseudonym "Publius Tacitus" on the website *Sic Temper Tyrannis* of well-known security analyst Pat Lang, alludes to the same kind of mirror-image perception trap. He writes that U.S. interference in Ukraine far overshadows anything that could be blamed on Russia. Recently released documents of the CIA show the close cooperation of the U.S. intelligence services with Stepan Bandera's Nazi-allied OUN since 1946. They show a history of collaboration, ranging from working with former president Viktor Yushchenko, whose wife was a senior official in the U.S. State Department and who declared Bandera to be a Ukrainian national hero,

to the direct cooperation with the Nazis in "Maidan II" and the coup against Ukrainian President Yanukovych in February 2014.

In fact, one can hardly find a greater distortion than the "narrative" regarding the events in Ukraine, which provides a large part of the basis for the demonization of Putin and Russia.

The same inability to recognize the new paradigm— President Xi Jinping's domestic and foreign policy, with its anti-corruption campaign, its absolute focus on scientific and technological innovation, and its "win-win" cooperation among nations in the New Silk Road Initiative—is manifest in the house organ of the British Empire, the *Economist*. Under the heading "How the West Got China Wrong," that journal laments the decision of the Central Committee to extend President Xi's term of office: "They hoped that economic integration would encourage China to evolve into a market economy and that, as they grew wealthier, its people would come to yearn for democratic freedoms, rights and the rule of law." Now, it seems, the West has completely misjudged China. According to the *Economist*, China is richer than anyone could have imagined, but instead of yearning to emulate the West, China is offering "Chinese wisdom and a Chinese approach to solving the problems facing mankind"! Blimey! London lost its bet!

And China recognizes that the one-party system works better than Western partisan conflict, while Chinese politics is profoundly influenced by traditional Chinese culture.

The West has not done its homework on Chinese history and culture, and should finally shake off its stereotypes about the second largest economy, reconciling its perception with China's reality. In the future, China will certainly deliver more surprises to the West, and make it even clearer that Beijing will never be a disciple of Washington.

And that's good! The reason Xi Jinping wants to continue his administration, lies in the recognition by the Chinese leadership that the coming years will be enormously important years of change for all humanity. As President Putin said in his speech, "This is a turning point for the whole world; and those who are willing and able to change, those who act and move forward will take the lead."

In fact, we are currently experiencing an epochal change. The period of nearly 600 years since the Italian Renaissance and the emergence of the sovereign nation-state, in which both oligarchic forms of government and governments committed to the common good existed side by side, is coming to an end. The new paradigm, a new phase in human evolution, is already visible. The closest approximation to this is Xi Jinping's vision of a "community of common destiny"—the concept that the idea of "one humanity" is set forth to all nations. The economic equivalent of this idea is the New Silk Road, in which all sovereign nations work together on the basis of cooperation for mutual benefit.

What we are currently experiencing, with all the unprovable accusations of "Russian hacking," "interference in democratic elections," "Chinese hegemony,"

The New York Stock Exchange.

"threats to the Western system of democracy and human rights by authoritarian systems," etc., is nothing more than a last gasp of a failing oligarchic system. The next financial collapse of this system—which has continually widened the gap between rich and poor, and whose policy of perpetual war has brought us both the refugee crisis and an epidemic of violence among young people and in the so-called entertainment industry—awaits us within a short interval, and will be worse than it was in 2008.

It is time for the rational people to reflect. We should use this new Sputnik shock and do what Putin says in his speech: "Let us sit down at the negotiating table and work together to design a new and relevant system of international security and sustainable development for all of human civilization."

The human species is the only creative species known to us. What sets us apart from all other beings, is the ability of the human mind to continually discover qualitatively new principles of the physical universe and apply them to the production process, thus improving the livelihood, productivity, and life expectancy of humanity. We have arrived at the point in history where we can and must realize our identity as a planetary species which is collectively capable of guaranteeing its long-term survival.

zepp-larouche@eir.de

EIR**Contents** www.larouchepub.com   Volume 45, Number 10, March 9, 2018

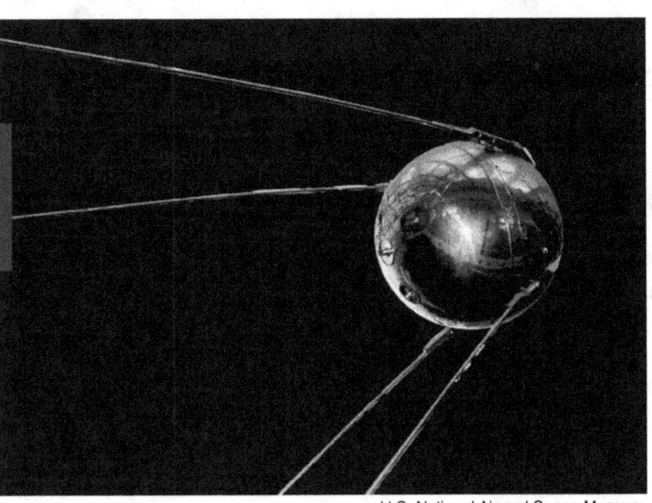

U.S. National Air and Space Museum

*Cover
This Week*

*A replica of
Sputnik 1.*

INTERNATIONAL CONFERENCE IN ABUJA

Conference on Lake Chad Is Historic Breakthrough for Development of Africa

by Claudio Celani

March 6—The International Conference on Lake Chad (ICLC), which met in the Nigerian capital of Abuja February 26-28, marked an historic breakthrough for Africa and globally. The conference adopted a road map ("The Charter of Abuja") towards a development plan centered around the most ambitious infrastructure program ever conceived for the African continent to reach this stage of implementation, and assigned the study of its feasibility to a joint Italian-Chinese venture. During the three-day conference, a new awareness and assertiveness emerged from African nations, inclining them to "think big" and take their destiny into their own hands, inspired by the formidable example of China's economic success. The conference also showed the emergence of a form of Europe-Africa-China tripartite cooperation that can be the model of international co-

https://statehouse.gov.ng/

A scene from the conference. When Nigerian President Muhammadu Buhari addressed the conference, he called for an urgent and immediate action plan by African leaders and the international community to reverse the ongoing drying out of the lake.

News Agency of Nigeria

From left: President Ali Bongo of Gabon; Chairman of the Heads of State and Government of the Lake Chad Basin Commission/President of Niger Republic Mahamadou Issoufou; President Muhammadu Buhari of Nigeria; President Idriss Déby Itno of Chad; and Faustin-Archange Touadéra of the Central African Republic, at the International Conference on Lake Chad in Abuja.

operation in the true spirit of China's Belt and Road Initiative.

The "Charter of Abuja," approved by eight African heads of state and government (see "Outcome of the Conference", page 12) asserts that saving Lake Chad from extinction is a pan-African imperative, that the only way to restore Lake Chad is through water transfer from the Congo basin, and that the most viable option for that transfer is the Transaqua project.

Transaqua, as our readers know, is the idea of a 2,400 km waterway intersecting all the right-side tributaries of the Congo River, from southern Congo to the watershed between the Central African Republic (CAR) and Chad, able to carry up to 100 billion cubic meters of water annually, thus restoring Lake Chad to its original surface area of 25,000 square km, regulating river flows, producing hydroelectric power, and offering major transport infrastructure connecting the Great Lakes region to the Sahel. Lyndon and Helga LaRouche and the Schiller Institutes have fought for this plan for almost thirty years, most of that time alongside the project's inventors at the Italian engineering firm Bonifica SpA.

The Italian firm Bonifica, which developed the idea

in the seventies, and the Chinese giant, PowerChina, have recently concluded a strategic alliance to conduct the feasibility study for Transaqua. At the Abuja conference, where the two companies presented the project, the Italian government announced that Italy will donate 1.5 million euros so that the feasibility study can begin.

This author accompanied the Bonifica delegation to the conference and took part in both public and closed-door sessions, as well as bilateral talks. My colleague Sébastien Périmony from the French Schiller Institute was also present as an observer, and helped maintain a high level in the discussions of the plenary session and the various panels. We also had the opportunity to give copies of the recent *Schiller Institute* report: *Extending the New Silk Road to West Asia and Africa* to various dignitaries, including the President and the Vice President of Nigeria, the President of Niger, and the Minister of Water Resources of Nigeria, who was the organizer of the conference, together with the Lake Chad Basin Committee (LCBC) and UNESCO.

To fully appreciate the importance of the decisions taken at the ICLC, one must know how dramatic the situation is in and around Lake Chad, where the existence of 40 million people is directly or indirectly threatened by the shrinking of the lake and by the proliferation of Boko Haram, the deadliest terror organization in the world.

The Lake Chad crisis is not new: it had already started in the Seventies. As LCBC outgoing executive secretary Sanusi Abdullahi stated in his introductory speech:

One proposal to transfer water from the Congo to Lake Chad called "Transaqua" was submitted to the LCBC in 1984 at the height of the most severe drought affecting the Lake Chad basin. This proposal was approved and shared by the then President Mobutu Sese Seko of Congo (former Zaire), but was considered too big,

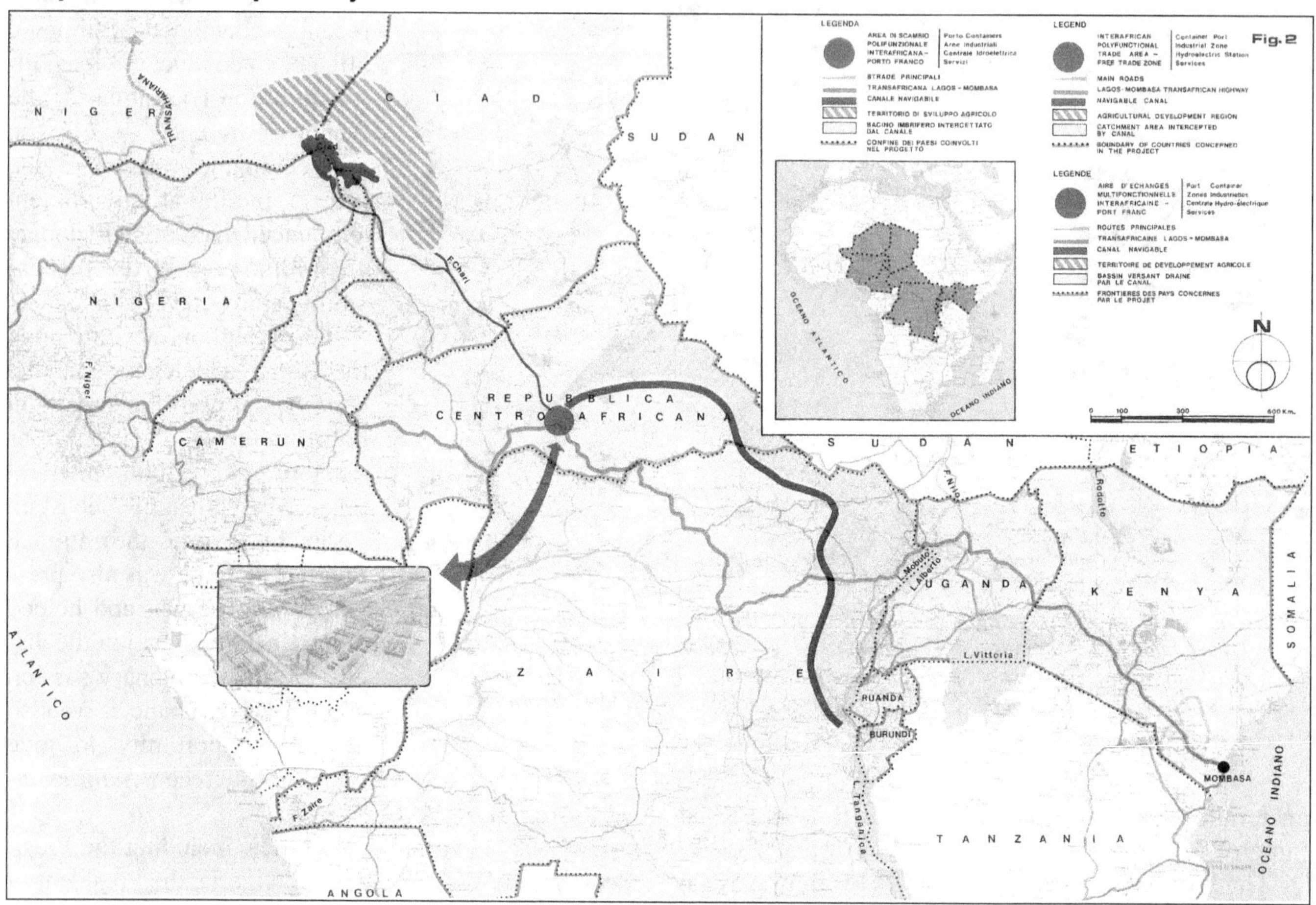

hence a smaller proposal taking water from the Ubangi River to Lake Chad was adopted by the Member States of the LCBC as requested by the Government of the Central African Republic.

Indeed, Transaqua is not "too big" if one considers, as Périmony noted in an intervention from the floor, that France has built 10,000 km of waterways; in comparison, the 2,400 km length of Transaqua is a "small" figure. The idea that Transaqua is "too big, and too expensive" has been pushed by those who want to keep Africa backward, and in a special way by one former European colonial power, whose influence on some member countries of the LCBC is still present and was even felt at the conference.

However, with the brilliant work done by the LCBC, the alliance between Bonifica and PowerChina, and the Italian decision allowing the feasibility study to begin, all hurdles were overcome.

As early as the first panel of the conference, featuring a presentation of the first project whose feasibility was explored by the LCBC, the Ubangi inter-basin water transfer project, it immediately became clear that there is no alternative to Transaqua. Mohammed Bila, a remote-sensing expert at the LCBC, gave a short but accurate report on the feasibility study conducted by the Canadian company CIMA, which concluded that the Ubangi water-transfer project was feasible, but (1) it would consume hydropower to pump the water uphill, while making no power available, and (2) the amount of water collected would raise the level of Lake Chad by a maximum of one meter.

So, Bila concluded, the Ubangi water-transfer project had been rejected by the LCBC, but it now considers Transaqua the only viable idea.

Transaqua Becomes the Focus

This presentation, done with scientific rigor and disarming candor, immediately shifted the focus onto Transaqua, even before the specific panel that had been

Italian Ambassador to Nigeria Addresses Final Plenary of Lake Chad Conference

movisol

Italian Ambassador to Nigeria, Stefano Pontesilli, makes a statement to the Lake Chad Conference.

March 3—After the formal greetings to authorities and dignitaries, Italian Ambassador Stefano Ponte-silli read the following speech:

We know the problem; we know the time to act is now; we have a possible solution. It is called Transaqua.

It is an idea for a water, transport, energy and agro-industrial development infrastructure for west-central Africa. It is a simple idea: to explore the possibility of collecting enough water from the northern tributaries of the Congo River, in order to refill Lake Chad and eventually develop hydroelectric power and irrigation. Bonifica calculated that refilling Lake Chad to its original dimensions would require an annual addition of approximately 50 billion cubic meters of water. Bonifica engineers envisioned the construction of a 2,400 km system of reservoirs and canals that would collect twice this amount, totaling approximately 5-8% of the Congo River water.

The Transaqua canal would start in the southeastern region of the Democratic Republic of Congo (DRC), intersects all tributaries upstream, across the DRC and the Central African Republic (CAR), and reach the watershed between the CAR and Chad at approximately 500 meters altitude. Here, it pours into the Chari River, Lake Chad's tributary, having carried 100 billion cubic meters of water per year by gravity alone in a 10-by-100-meter canal. It will be a really a new, manmade river, with dimensions and flow comparable to the Nile at the Aswan Dam.

Along its path, Transaqua will create systems of reservoirs, water regulation, and hydropower production, benefitting every basin of the Congo tributaries, without negatively affecting their carrying capacity, fisheries, or navigability. Furthermore, a road will be built as necessary to serve the construction of the canal-dam system, which will remain as a modern transport connection in central Africa. The canal itself will be a magnificent waterway; and plans en-vision building at least one major inland port and economic development area in the CAR.

We all know the benefits for the countries surrounding the Lake Chad basin, but let me dwell for a minute on the benefits for the CAR and DRC, which are not directly affected by the drought in the Sahel.

Transaqua will provide significant infrastructure. These two countries will indeed be major beneficiaries of the project, as they will have a waterway, hydropower, a road, and the benefits of productive employment and work experience for a large workforce over several years.

Ladies and gentlemen, the Italian government has expressed interest in the project. This is why: we believe that Transaqua addresses the root causes of the economic desperation that forces people living in the area to emigrate to Europe. It also gives a very concrete meaning to the proposals of launching a "Marshall Plan" to create jobs and development in the immigrants' countries of origin, some of them coming from the Sahel region.

To this effect, the Italian government has decided to pledge up to 1.5 million euros for the feasibility study for the Transaqua project. Thank you.

Coverage and video of the ambassador's remarks are posted to the website of Movisol, the International Civil Rights Solidarity Movement, the co-thinkers of Lyndon and Helga LaRouche in Italy, under the title: "L'ambasciatore italiano in Nigeria: l'Italia crede nel progetto."

Schiller Institute

Dr. Matthew Adepoju (second from left) and other members of the team from the Nigerian Space Research and Development Agency (NASRDA). Dr. Adepoju, the head of Cadastral Mapping and Urban Space Applications for NASRDA, was a session chair. Also present are Sébastien Périmony of the Schiller Institute, France (third from left), and a journalist from Nigeria Magazine *(second from right).*

planned for it was held the following day. That panel on Transaqua included presentations by Bonifica and PowerChina. Many interventions from the podium and the audience showed strong support for the "big" project, and in some cases an astonishing degree of detailed knowledge of Transaqua.

For example, the next day, when a representative from Congo addressed the plenary session expressing solidarity with the Chad basin countries, but offering a list of reservations motivated by Congo's aspiration to follow in the footsteps of African Unity pioneer Kwame Nkrumah, discussant Abubakar Bobboi Jauro replied that "the Transaqua idea was developed by the Italian firm Bonifica exactly in the spirit of Nkrumah's vision."

Then, when the breakout session with Bonifica technical director Franco Bocchetto and PowerChina deputy chief engineer Huang Ziping finally took place, there was a packed room with people standing in the back. In presenting Transaqua, Bocchetto showed, among other things, that the CIMA study presented by Engineer Bila had concluded that a dam on the Kotto River (a tributary of the Ubangi), would allow water-transfer to cross the divide with the Bamingui, a tributary of the Logone/Chari and therefore of Lake Chad, by gravity, exactly "at the end of the route of the Transaqua project."

By itself, the dam on the Kotto River could provide a limited amount of water transfer and have an insubstantial impact on the Lake Chad equilibrium. "But it represents the first link of a chain of similar reservoirs on the other tributaries of the Ubangi and Congo, to be connected by canals to form the Transaqua waterway."

The priority stretch in the Central African Republic can be implemented by steps, each providing immediate local benefits: hydropower, irrigation, or flow regulation.

Mr. Bocchetto was followed by Mr. Huang, who showed and commented upon a video on the Central Route of China's South-North Water Transfer Project, a 1,400 km canal built by PowerChina to bring water from the Yangtse River to the Beijing region. Combined, the two presentations had a powerful impact: on one side, the project which critics scoff at as "pharaonic"; on the other side the demonstration that a similar "pharaonic" project has in fact been realized.

During the discussion, the PowerChina engineer answered a question from the audience by explaining that, although several years will elapse between the feasibility study and the completion of the project, we will not wait until the waterway is finished to "open the tap" and begin to re-fill Lake Chad. Water will start to flow as soon as the first dam is built—i.e. the last one on the route, the Kotto dam in the Central African Republic.

I intervened to announce that financing for the feasibility study had been secured. The Italian ambassador had told LCBC Executive Secretary Sanusi Abdullahi that the Italian government would provide half of the cost of the study—the other half to be supplied by PowerChina. The ambassador would announce that officially the next day, at the final plenary session.

In addition, I suggested that although Africans are quite right in considering the Lake Chad issue to be pan-African, yet the solution being considered also places a global responsibility on them. It is global because the emerging Italian-Chinese alliance to restore Lake Chad can become a model for successful Europe-China-Africa tripartite cooperation in the spirit of Chi-

Selected Press Coverage

The strategic importance of the Bonifica-PowerChina alliance was not missed by the international media present at the conference. A few hours later, AFP ran a report, published by many outlets in French and English, titled: "Italy, China propose solution to Lake Chad water's problem" , while Radio France International (RFI) interviewed *EIR*'s Claudio Celani.

Too ambitious, too risky, too expensive? The reasons to oppose it are not lacking, but the project to fill Lake Chad is back. On Tuesday, Feb. 27 in Abuja, Nigeria, the titanic ambition to transfer the waters of the Congo Basin was on everyone's lips, as reported by the Italian analyst Claudio Celani:

"People here are very convinced that water transfer is the only way to revitalize Lake Chad. They see big things. They understand that they need a big project, Transaqua, the big project that is intended not only to move water from point A to point B, but also to build a real modern infrastructure in the heart of Africa," he explains.

RFI continues: "Transaqua is being reborn from its ashes. The Italian company Bonifica at the origin of the project, is now associated with the Chinese company PowerChina. A joint feasibility study will be funded by the Chinese and Italian governments. PowerChina's chief engineer is pleased with this collaboration: 'I believe we are at the beginning of a new cooperation. We look forward to starting this cooperation.'"

AFP quotes Lake Chad Basin Commission Executive Secretary Sanusi Abdullahi:

"Inter-basin water transfer is not an option but a necessity. We are faced with the possibility of Lake Chad disappearing, and that would be catastrophic to the entire African continent."

Technical director Franco Bocchetto of the Italian engineering firm Bonifica, which first designed the Transaqua project some 35 years ago, is quoted, "The vision of hundreds of people dying in the Mediterranean Sea" had spurred the Italian government to support the project. "In recent years the situation has rapidly changed, and what did not seem possible in the '80s has become of interest."

AFP continues, " 'We work here for projects and we want to take social responsibility,' said Ziping Huang, an engineer at PowerChina."

In a report on the Abuja conference headlined "Italy, China Ponder 2,400 km Canal To Save Lake Chad," the London-based *Global Construction Review* includes a map from the Schiller Institute showing the extent of the project: "One version of the plan would involve damming a tributary [sic] of the River Congo in the Central African Republic and digging a 2,400-km-long canal to the River Chari, which feeds Lake Chad. A talk on the project given by Franco Persio Bocchetto, a director of Bonifica, to the Schiller Institute can be seen," and the article provides the hyperlink to Bocchetto's November 2017 speech at the Schiller Institute conference in Bad Soden, Germany.

Left to right: Conference participants Sébastien Périmony (Schiller Institute France), Franco Bocchetto (technical director Bonifica), Romina Boldrini (CEO Bonifica), Claudio Celani, and Ercole Incalza (foreign director, Bonifica).

na's Belt and Road Initiative. It is no secret that there is strong opposition to the Belt and Road in the West, and it must be defeated. The tripartite alliance for Transaqua is the best way to show that a win- win model is possible.

The moderator suggested that this proposition be included in the official record, along with other ideas emerging from the panel.

Later on, the same two speakers, Bocchetto and Huang, made a joint presentation during the closed-door session of the Council of Ministers of the LCBC.

The final day of the conference opened with the High Level Session, with the presence of Muhammadu Buhari, President of the Federal Republic of Nigeria; Issoufou Mahamadou, President of the Republic of Niger and Acting President of the LCBC; Idriss Déby, President of the Republic of Chad; Ali Bongo Ondingba, President of the Republic of Gabon; Faustin-Archange Touadéra, President of the Central African Republic; and Filhomé Nyang, Prime Minister of Cameroon, representing President Paul Biya.

A problem emerged during the report on the plenary sessions and the breakout sessions, read by the official rapporteur. In contrast to the general thrust of the conference, the report on the breakout session with Bonifica and PowerChina censored the entire content, including the speakers and even the theme of the session. This prompted the moderator, LCBC scientific board deputy chairman Lawrence Freeman, to call on the rapporteur to correct his report, because it did not reflect the fact that Transaqua had been the leading issue in at least three panels.

Thereafter the Road Map was presented by Prof. Salihu Mustafa. It included the indication that Transaqua is the preferred solution for Lake Chad, and that a $50 billion Lake Chad Fund should be created to finance water transfer and infrastructure (see box1_page XX).

The final session, chaired by the Nigerian deputy foreign minister, was concluded with an address by Italian Ambassador Stefano Pontesilli (see box 2_page XX). His announcement of a grant for the Transaqua feasibility study was received with strong applause. Both the Nigerian deputy foreign minister and its water resource minister officially commended Italy for its support.

As Schiller Institute founder Helga Zepp-LaRouche summed it up afterwards, "This is *really* good news for anyone who cares about the human species."

Outcome of the Conference

March 6—These are excerpts from the final version of the Road Map approved at the International Conference on Lake Chad, Abuja, February 26-28, 2018.

- The various studies carried out show that there is no solution to the shrinking of Lake Chad that does not involve recharging the lake by transfer of water from outside the basin.
- That Inter-basin water transfer is not an option; but a necessity.
- That failure to appropriate and timely action, will result in Lake Chad completely drying up soon, and that would cause humanitarian crisis and pose serious security challenges, not only for the region, but for the entire African continent and the World.
- The Transaqua Project which would take water from the right tributar[ies] of River Congo, conveying the water 2,400 km channel to Chari River is the preferred feasible option.
  - Consider the consequences of Lake Chad disappearing not only as a regional issue but, an African tragedy.
  - Endorse the Inter-basin Water Transfer (IBWT) initiative as a Pan-African project
    - To restore the Lake for peace and security to reign in the Lake Chad region and
    - The promotion of navigation, industrial and economic development in the whole Congo basin.
- The African Development Bank to facilitate the creation of the Lake Chad Fund of USD 50 billion, to be sourced from African States and donations by Africa's Development Partners to fund the Lake Chad IBWT and infrastructure projects.

Strategy: Short Term Goals

- Review and adopt implementation plan for restoration and revitalization of Lake Chad
- Ameliorating security threat
- De-silting, weeding and river training of rivers flowing into the lake
- Explore the possibility of rain water catchment alter-

Participants in a session of the Lake Chad Conference.

Schiller Institute

native water scheme within the basin

- Build capacity of LCBC and Stakeholder Institutions through collaborative arrangements with regional capacity building networks
- Establish hydrologic and hydrogeological data networks and develop research to understand the hydrodynamics of the Lake
- Undertake studies to establish the hydraulic conductivity of the Nubian sandstone aquifer with the basin
- Finalize the ongoing feasibility study of Transaqua Project
- Conduct baseline survey of bio-diversity of the basin to develop a genetic data bank of plant and animal species in the basin
- Conduct an Environmental Impact Assessment study of the preferre option for restoring the Lake with corresponding Environmental and Social Management Plan (ESMP)
- Develop and implement a communication strategy for the restoration of the lake
- Review and implement a Master Plan for Lake Chad
- Initiate the process for raising the $50 billion Lake Chad Fund

- Establish social mobilization and strengthen communication strategy to involve stakeholders, promote publicity, raise awareness and education on rational water use and environment management
- Advocacy for sustainable use of water resources and environmental restoration
- Strenghten local and regional partnerships amongst existing institutions, viz LCBC/CISCO.

Strategy: Medium and Long Term Goals

Medium Term Goals
- Produce detail design of the preferred project
- Implement ESMP of the preferred option for restoration of the Lake
- Explore the possibility of utilizing the abundant ground water reserve in the basin
- Develop and undertake catchment management of Logone-Chari and Congo watersheds and integrate with existing Kyobe and Yedseram/Ngadda CMP
- Develop and implement afforestation and greening programme of the Lake Chad basin to reduce evaporation loss
- Promote ecological and biodiversity advancement.

Long Term Goals
- Undertake the development of the Lake Chad to transform its environment for economic growth and stability of the region
- Implement the integrated catchment management plan for the watersheds.

Financing Strategy
- Secure the $50 Billion Lake Chad Fund
- Adopt Tariff, Taxes and Transfer (3Ts) funding approach Explore social and economic principles, where Social component of project is funded through public sources (from riparian countries: commitment must be higher than the existing level) and Economic component is funded using public funds and loans.

A Victory in Abuja

This is an edited transcript of the March 1, 2018 Schiller Institute New Paradigm webcast interview of the founder of the Schiller Institutes, Helga Zepp-LaRouche. She was interviewed by Harley Schlanger. A video of the webcast will be available.

Harley Schlanger: Hello. I'm Harley Schlanger from the Schiller Institute. Welcome to today's international strategic webcast, featuring our founder, Helga Zepp-La-Rouche.

We have some really big news to report to start the program, which comes from Abuja, the capital of Nigeria, the site of a conference focussed on a project that's near and dear to our hearts, a project that Helga's been fighting for over many years. Helga, report on what happened in Abuja.

Helga Zepp-LaRouche: It is really fantastic that this conference took place in Abuja with the participation of the Nigerian government and the Lake Chad Basin Commission (LCBC) and the other members of the LCBC in addition to Nigeria: Cameroon, Chad, Niger, Algeria, Central African Republic, Libya, and Sudan. They officially adopted the Transaqua project. A communiqué issued at the close of the conference announced the participants' agreement that the only solution to the Lake Chad crisis is to bring water from outside the Lake Chad basin by building the Transaqua project.

Let me quickly explain what this is: If it is carried out, it will be the largest infrastructure project, I think, in all of history. This idea was first developed in the 1970s, by the Italian engineering firm Bonifica, to take 3-4% of the water from some of the tributaries of the Congo River, which is now flowing unused into the Atlantic, and redirect it instead from a point 500 m above sea level, through a system of canals into Lake Chad. This will work very well, because of the difference in height of flow, so it will be a very efficient system. It would not just refill Lake Chad, which is obviously an absolutely urgent necessity, because this lake has been

EIRNS

The Conference on Lake Chad, held in Abuja, Nigeria, and attended by five presidents, adopted Transaqua.

drying out—only 10% of its original surface area is left. Poverty, which has been increasing because of the growing lack of water, has given rise to the terrorist Boko Haram, which is one of the reasons why all the countries participating in this project now say that it's not an option, but a necessity. If you don't realize such a development program, you may as well hand over the whole territory to the Boko Haram.

This project would refill Lake Chad, making plenty of water available for irrigation of the Sahel zone. It would give water to all participating countries—but not only water, it would build modern infrastructure in the heart of Africa. It would create an inland waterway for these countries for shipping as well as generating much needed hydropower generation of electricity.

This is really, really fantastic. The Schiller Institute has been campaigning for this project as part of our World Land-Bridge. Even earlier, we started to hold conferences on this in the beginning of the 1990s, working with the engineers from Bonifica: it's really our work. There was an article in *People's Daily* last year, which said that this connection between PowerChina—the Chinese engineering and construction firm—and Bonifica is really thanks to the work of the Schiller Institute. So, I'm very happy that this is happening.

At the conference, the Italian Ambassador to Nigeria proudly announced that the Italian government will fund more than half of the cost of the feasibility study, which is now going to go into motion. All of the people involved are completely passionate about this idea, they were happy, really happy about the conclusions reached.

We had two members of the Schiller Institute participating as guests at the conference: Claudio Celani, who's Italian, who has done good work on all of this, and also one of our French members, Sébastien Périmony. Celani pointed out in discussion at the conference that this is not just infrastructure, this is not just two countries working together for the first time, but that this can be a model for the New Paradigm of cooperation by means of the New Silk Road; China working with Italy, a European country, and this Chinese-Italian collaboration working together with African nations on this very far-reaching project.

I think this is really fantastic and I'm absolutely convinced this will work very well. Bonifica is an extremely efficient company as is PowerChina—they both have great expertise. PowerChina built the Three Gorges Dam. They have a lot of experience with such large earth-moving and similar kinds of technologies. So, this is really, really good!

These kinds of projects provide a perspective for solving the refugee crisis: that is exactly what is needed. You have to get the young people involved in building such projects. As the President of Ghana said in a trip to Germany this week, in 20 years, Africa will have 2 billion people—you will need a lot of jobs, and a lot of education. The President of Ghana on an earlier occasion emphasized that these young people should be able to work to build the continent, rather than fleeing through the Sahara and drowning in the Mediterranean: he wants to reverse that, and that is why he wants investment, not development aid. This is an example of exactly how it can be done.

This is *really* good news, for anybody who cares about the human species.

Schlanger: Helga, you mentioned that this is a realization of the New Paradigm. A couple of weeks ago at an Africa Day event in Berlin, I was talking to a number of African ambassadors about this. One of them said,

"Transaqua, that's big. We need big. We don't need people to tell us to be small any more. We need big projects. We need to leapfrog."

This is in the context of the overall advance of the New Silk Road dynamic. There's been a lot of discussion in China about projects that are under way. Why don't you fill us in on what's going on from China on this?

Zepp-LaRouche: I think the Silk Road spirit is really catching on. At the recent Dubai Global Business Forum, for example, in Dubai, the President of Panama, in an interview with Xinhua, strongly endorsed the Belt and Road Initiative. He said he wants Panama to be a part of it. An agreement has been reached with China to build a high-speed railway system between Panama and Costa Rica as a first step to connect Central America with Asia in a much more productive way.

Almost every day we have new developments. Several Chinese professors commented that the Belt and Road Initiative is not just for China, but it will uplift the whole world. This approach provides a model for all developing countries to improve their industrial base, and all the neighbors of China will also do so. Another professor who has written several books on the New Silk Road, Prof. Yang Yiwei, said the reason the West is so full of anxiety about the rise of China is because there is a complete lack of economic self-confidence in the West. That is why there is so much hysteria about China.

Then there was a very beautiful interview with Su Quanke. He is the chief engineer of the Hong Kong-Zhuhai-Macao Bridge, which is now completed. It includes a very long tunnel that reduces the travel time between Hong Kong and Zhuhai from three hours to only 30 minutes. He was asked if he was optimistic that China could reach its development goals in 2020, 2035, and 2050. He said he was absolutely certain that these goals would be met.

This bridge is really fantastic. I had the good fortune to be on the bridge at the end of November—I was invited to a Maritime Silk Road conference in Zhuhai. Part of the program was to travel over the bridge. I was only 15 km from Hong Kong and it was fantastic. It's the longest sea bridge on the planet. I think it's altogether 55 km long. To construct it, 150 new patents were needed, all of which were invented by Chinese engineers.

This region—the Hong Kong, Macao, Zhuhai, Guangzhou, Shenzhen region—is probably *the* powerhouse of the world economy by now. All it's cities are modern, with relatively beautiful architecture—I was really surprised to see that—it's a powerhouse attracting young, creative people in the high-tech areas. This is the kind of example, where you see that with modern infrastructure, such development becomes a magnet: everything flourishes around it.

I hope that we in the West, including in the United States, could do exactly the same thing! I recently saw an article that asked if "the United States could have a 7% growth rate, like China?"

The just completed, 55-km Hong Kong-Zhuhai-Macao Bridge connects the three cities on the Pearl River Delta.

The answer was, yes, it could, *if* the United States would go back to the economic policies of Alexander Hamilton, which after all is what China is now doing! China is basing its own model on Alexander Hamilton and Friedrich List, and other such proponents of physical economy. The theories of my husband are also quite well known in China and I think they are also being studied very intensively.

This is all very, very good, and there is absolute reason for optimism.

Schlanger: And this brings up the broader scope of Chinese diplomacy. Liu He is going to the United States. He's one of China's chief economists. He'll be meeting with people in Washington. What do you expect will come from this trip?

Zepp-LaRouche: I think it is very interesting. There is clearly an effort by President Xi and President Trump to collaborate. The good news is that Xi will now remain President beyond 2020, which has caused great hysteria in some quarters, but I think it's a very good development. Clearly, the Chinese people appreciate his successes in the anti-corruption fight and the New Silk Road and the Belt and Road Initiative is a *huge* success. Trump has announced that he will run again in 2020. And therefore, I think it's very important that the two presidents continue the policy of having direct contact with each other, and in that way bypass some of the neocon loudmouths and the efforts to destabilize the relationship between China and the United States.

The economist Liu He was the main speaker for China at the World Economic Forum in Davos, Switzerland. He is also the most important economic advisor to President Xi. The Davos Forum took place only two weeks after State Councilor Yang Jiechi was in the United States, meeting with Trump and other officials. The personal relationship between Trump and Xi is functioning well, and this is a very important counter to much of the other nonsense and anti-China hysteria that is being pushed right now.

Schlanger: On the question of anti-China hysteria, we have to take a look at this new report from the Center for Strategic and International Studies (CSIS), which just came out last week. It claims that China is planning cruise missile strikes on Washington that will assassinate U.S. leaders, and that China is also planning to invade Taiwan. This is a further escalation of what we've seen in the last weeks. What's going on with this, Helga?

Zepp-LaRouche: This is an example of what General Dempsey, the previous Chairman of the U.S. Joint Chiefs of Staff, had warned of: the "Thucydides trap." This describes a situation in which the dominant power, now the United States, thinks that it is confronted with the rise of a new power, China, in this case, and that the United States thinks it must continue to dominate China. If the United States were to follow such crazy scenarios as that advanced by CSIS, it would fall into the Thucydides trap.

Thucydides was the Greek historian who described how the Peloponnesian War developed out of the rivalry between Athens and Sparta and how that conflict led to the demise of ancient Greece. So, if the United States were to fall into this trap of confrontation, it would be absolutely terrible. China has frequently put forward a new kind of relationship among the great powers. It has offered to cooperate with the United States in the win-win policy of the New Silk Road. So this utopian CSIS claim is really stupid. Similar to its line against China, CSIS claims that Russia could make a surprise attack in the Baltics. That has *no* logic whatsoever. It is absolutely not in the self-interest of Russia to do that. And anybody who knows the situation can see that very clearly.

© World Economic Forum/Sandra Blaser

Economist Liu He, speaking at the World Economic Forum, Davos, Jan. 24, 2018.

There was a very powerful answer to this study in *Global Times*, which points out that the United States is being frightened by its own mirror image. *Global Times* then quotes a utopian from the Pentagon Office of Net Assessment, who developed all these airpower policies, Andrew Marshall. He had coined this notion of a "mirror image," meaning that countries will often mistakenly project their own strategy onto the supposed intention of other nations. That's exactly what the United States is doing, reports the *Global Times*. Who is pushing pre-emptive war? That is the doctrine of the United States, not that of China. Who has been pushing regime change? It's the United States, while the policy of China always has been to respect other countries' sovereignty. The article continues with several other such comparisons. This CSIS study is really bad. People should really not fall for it because anybody who studies history knows the horrible consequences of such an approach.

There is also the danger of charges by Marco Rubio and others, alleging that the Confucius Institutes spy on U.S. colleges—it's all absolute paranoia. In China today, you have a very successful approach, which is lifting many of the underdeveloped parts of the world out of poverty. China is, however,

CSIS: China and Russia are enemies of the U.S., waiting to pounce.

absolutely not trying to impose its own model on other countries.

The United States could go back to its own successful periods, like the American Revolution, Lincoln, John Quincy Adams, Franklin D. Roosevelt, and John F. Kennedy. If the United States were to go back to its own strength and the European nations back to our best traditions, we would not be importing the Chinese model; we would be regaining our own true identities again. But since the West is not doing that, some people are indeed worried about China—but that perspective is really, absolutely wrong.

Schlanger: And we saw the same thing at the hearing at which Marco Rubio made his crazy remarks. At that same hearing, FBI Director Christopher Wray basically said that every Chinese student studying in the United States is a potential spy. So this is something worse than the McCarthy era.

On that same theme, we've seen recently, a very difficult rough patch in U.S.-Russian relations. Now, with the dangers of an explosion about Syria—with people blaming Russia and saying the Assad regime is allegedly planning a possible chemical weapons attack—Russian foreign minister Lavrov had some comments on this: He called on the United States to back the UN Security Council resolution for humanitarian aid in Syria. What's going on there, from what you see, Helga?

Zepp-LaRouche: After the Russian intervention in September 2015, the Syrian territory was basically re-conquered, step by step. Now you have very few enclaves controlled by al-Qaeda-related groups. One of them is the suburb of Damascus, Eastern Ghouta. To get an idea of what is going on now in Syria, think of it this way: If you were to have in the German city of Potsdam or the Schwabing district, thousands of ISIS fighters shelling the inner cities of Berlin or Munich, or if there were ISIS fighters in New Jersey shelling New York City, what would be the reaction? Government has the absolute right to try to stop such violent attacks. These terrorists, in Syria, are keeping the whole population hostage. Now, thanks to Putin's intervention, it became possible to have five-hour corridor ceasefires every day. The world is now witness to the fact that these terrorist forces are trying to prevent those individuals and families trapped in Ghouta from leaving—the terrorists are using those people as human shields behind whom they can hide.

The accusations of the West—some Western powers are still advocating the policy of regime change; this was the policy of the European Union, of the German government, and of the British government. This is absolutely wrong.

I do not think regime change will succeed, but these policies just escalate the suffering of the Syrian people, and I think it cannot, it will not, work, because the forces now backing the Assad sovereign government have proven to be militarily superior. But it's a terrible tragedy and it should stop immediately.

Schlanger: We've had a new debate in the United States following the killings—the tragedy—that took place at the Parkland high school in Florida. There was a very interesting intervention by the Governor of Kentucky, Matthew Bevin, who made the comment that what we're looking at is a "culture of death." I think the theme that you've taken up with the Schiller Institute over many years, about the necessity to address the cultural degeneration which is directly related to warfare, is a key point to bring up. So I'd like you to present your thoughts on this. It is at the heart of a lot of the discussion in the United States, but it's not a local issue, it's part of the overall degeneration of the culture.

Zepp-LaRouche: Many, many years ago, I gave a speech about the dangers of Pokémon, the danger of certain violent movies, the danger of video games. At that point, I looked at it, and it was very clear that some of these videos came directly from the Pentagon's strategic studies and training programs. In the post-war period, people realized that during World War II only 15% of the soldiers were willing to shoot at the enemy. There is a natural block in people about shooting another human being. The aim of these video games initially was to increase the army kill rate, and they then became the basis for commercial video games. This has

now reached a new degree of violence, violence for the sake of violence. Coleen Rowley, a member of the Veteran Intelligence Professionals for Sanity (VIPS), talking about the Parkland shootings, pointed out that the Pentagon and the CIA have, in the last several years, worked directly with Hollywood on 1,800 movies that have a hero who is some kind of deranged person, some military veteran with post-traumatic stress disorder, running around in killing sprees, and that this has been a significant contributing factor in this present explosion of violence.

My husband, Lyndon LaRouche, made extremely important comments after the Columbine high school shootings that occurred in 1999: he brought attention to the deep, deep axiomatic cultural danger to the United States that was exposed by this event. Since Columbine, there have been 38 school shootings with fatal consequences. After the Parkland shooting, there were 50 alarms in schools per day—obviously, pupils being concerned about other pupils, or weapons, or having strange social messages. I think this is really reaching a point where this has to change.

It's very good that President Trump made some extremely important comments on that: He met with some of the pupils from the Parkland school and he said there is terrible violence, a lot of it on the Internet, which is shaping the minds of young people. He is considering a rating system for movies, which may not have sex and therefore are not rated, but are full of killing.

I think this is a step in the right direction but it is not enough. I would really go for a much more radical approach and propose legislation forbidding any such movies because they contribute to the menticide of children. People have argued in the past that you can't block the violence on the Internet. I think you can. Some people criticize China for blocking certain things on the Internet—if the Chinese can do that, so could the West, to protect its own youth and children.

I think this is a very important. As I have said many times: The New Paradigm is not just about economics and the New Silk Road is not just concerned with transportation or infrastructure. The New Paradigm will also develop a completely new conception of the human being. The kind of bestialization, the absolute, terrible lack of dignity of the human person that Governor Bevin of Kentucky pointed out, is really the exact opposite of what is needed. We need a beautiful image of man, an image which is creative, which is truthful, and which develops all the potentials of each child in the fullest possible way.

President Trump (left) met students from the Parkland, Fla., high school after the mass shooting.

Many people who have tolerated this degeneracy have, at the same time, stoked hysteria about China's system of giving advantages to people whose behavior is in the interest of the common good, while giving negative points to people who don't do that. There is a big debate, at least in Europe, about that. People are absolutely upset about it. However, after some discussion, we came to the conclusion that in Europe and the Americas similar systems have existed for a long time: we in the West just describe it differently. Even in Germany, which is not the worst place, 25% of all teenagers are regarded by industry as absolutely unemployable. They won't be hired, they won't get apprenticeships because they're not motivated, they're autistic, they're just not fit—so they have no chance of getting jobs. This is certainly a selective system as well!

Is this really the Western system, where everything is allowed, everything goes? You have not two sexes, or three sexes, by now you have something like 49 genders. Is it really acceptable, given that the drug epidemic in the United States has led to a decrease in the expected lifespan? Governor Bevin pointed out that some of these satanic messages are in the lyrics of the pop music, in the movies, in the video games—should we allow all of this and have our society be completely destroyed? There is an effect from all of this on the cognitive powers!

The Four Laws of Lyndon LaRouche are the only solution to prevent a collapse of the system. The Fourth Law demands a crash program for fusion power, for international space research and travel. If you want this to work, you can't do it with young people who are destroying their minds, who are hooked on these things. We need these young people to become a creative, productive labor power.

So it's one and the same discussion, which is needed—we need a New Paradigm, and we have to have an education system that emphasizes the beauty of Classical culture, which emphasizes the beauty of the character as a development goal. This was an idea of Wilhelm von Humboldt, who after all, influenced much of the education system in Europe and the United States in the 19th Century, and his ideas lasted over a large part of the 20th Century. His idea was that the aim of education must be the beauty of character. Who talks about that these days? If you go to some of these kids who are hooked on these violent video games, or even look at terrible material on the Internet which displays the use of torture and similar things, their minds are being destroyed!

So, since Governor Bevin asked for a national debate about that, and fortunately, since President Trump also wants to take on this issue, let us have a debate. In my view, we must have a debate on this because we can't let this continue. Solving this crisis is an integral part of the United States joining the New Paradigm and the New Silk Road. For many years, the Schiller Institute has proven that with Classical music, with Classical poetry, with Schiller, with Shakespeare, you can transform people and have an aesthetical education. That is exactly what is needed right now.

Schlanger: Helga, I think coming back to where we started, introducing projects such as the Transaqua project will give millions of young Africans a sense of the future. I would encourage people to go to the Schiller Institute site, and get a copy of the special report we have on that: "Extending the New Silk Road to West Asia and Africa: A Vision of an Economic Renaissance" which is now available.

So, Helga, with that, I'd like to thank you again for joining us, and we'll see you next week.

Zepp-LaRouche: Yes, till next week.

Moving Water: By Land and by Air

by Mike Billington

March 5—China's water problem is in one sense the opposite of that in the United States. In North America, the northwest regions of Alaska and Canada's far west receive an abundance of precipitation, while the U.S. southwest and northern Mexico are water-starved. It is the opposite in China—the southeast region in the Yangtze River basin has abundant fresh water resources, while the northeast, which holds a large portion of the nation's population, industry, and arable land, is desperately short of water.

But the big difference is that China is dealing with this imbalance, by moving water from the south to the north, while the United States has done nothing to resolve its problem, and thus suffers periodic droughts, resulting in recurring economic and social disasters. The North American Water and Power Alliance (NAWAPA), promoted by President Kennedy, would have moved Alaskan water south to the West and Southwest of the United States, and into northern Mexico—it would have been the largest infrastructure program ever undertaken by mankind. But like most large-scale scientific and infrastructural projects in the United States, NAWAPA died with JFK and his brother.

China, on the other hand, has unleashed the most massive water-moving program in human history, which is already partially in service and doing its job on behalf of current and future generations. The South-North Water Transfer Project (SNWTP) is China's multi-pronged Great Project to move water from the Yangtze River in the South to the Yellow River region in the North. Mao Zedong set in motion a feasibility study for such a project during a tour of the Yellow River region in 1952. It took 50 years until the plan was launched in 2002.

There are three canal routes which, when completed, will together move 44 cubic km/yr of water to the North. For comparison, the Yangtze disgorges on

china.org.cn

Central route starting-point Taocha in Xichuan County, Nanyang, Henan Province. Looking "upstream," toward the Danjiangkou Reservoir.

The Caohe River Aqueduct.

average nearly 1,000 cu. km/yr into the East China Sea, while the Yellow River's average is only 8 cu. km/yr. The severity of the water crisis in Beijing, with a population of 24.9 million in its metropolitan area, is such that the huge amount of water to be transferred by the SNWTP will only meet about one third of the need for this rapidly growing region. Other means, including massive desalination plants, are also being developed.

The total combined length of the planned canals, is nearly 4,350 km, the approximate distance from New York to Los Angeles. The three routes are:

• The *Eastern Route* which follows the ancient Beijing-Hangzhou Grand Canal route, was built between the 5th Century BC and the 6th Century AD to carry grain from the South to the North. When completed, the Eastern Route will deliver 14.8 cu. km/yr of water from the Yangtze River, near its point of discharge into the East China Sea, north to Tianjin, 108 km southeast of Beijing. The Eastern Route was partially opened in December 2013. Pumping stations move the water along the uphill route, while a tunnel carries the water under the Yellow River, and from there, an aqueduct carries the water to reservoirs near Tianjin.

• The *Central Route*, completed in December 2014, moves water from the Han River tributary of the Yangtze, from a reservoir at Danjiangkou in Hubei Province, to the capital of Beijing and nearby Tianjin. The existing dam at Danjiangkou was raised by 13 meters, allowing the water to flow downhill into the canal, and then flow through the 1,400

South-North Water Diversion Project

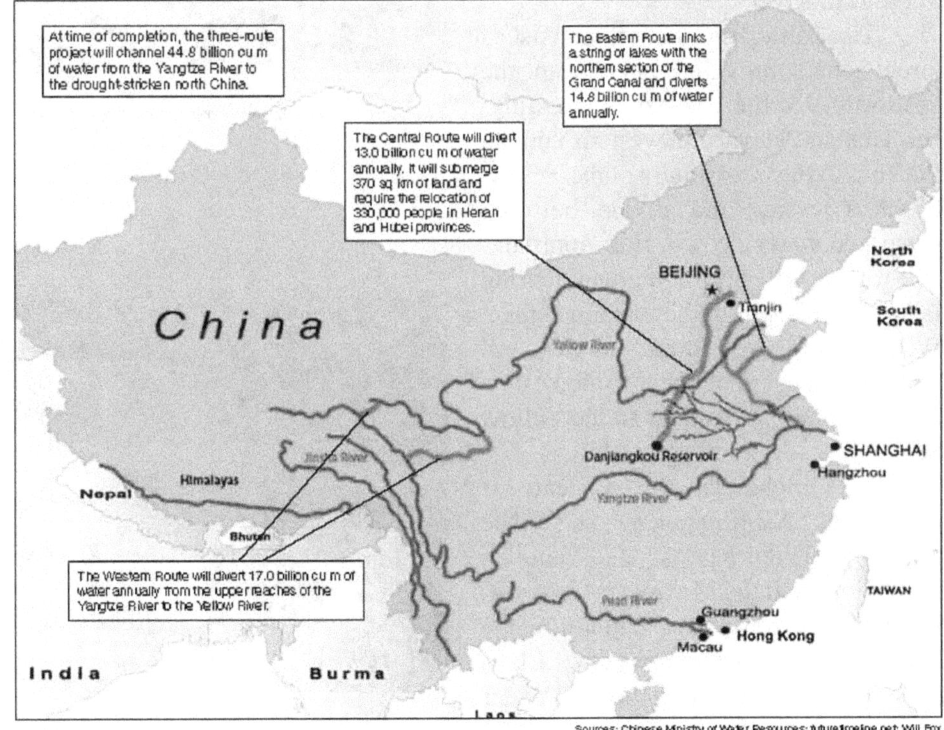

Sources: Chinese Ministry of Water Resources; futuretimeline.net; Will Fox

km route to Beijing entirely by gravity. This is the longest canal in the world, although the planned canal to move water from the Congo River to replenish Lake Chad in the African Sahel, will be still longer, at 2,500 km. (A feasibility study for the Lake Chad project is being conducted by Italy's Bonifica SpA and China's PowerChina: see article, page 6.)

The initial flow through the Central Route provides 9.5 cu. km to Beijing annually, but this will increase to 13 cu. km by 2030. Twin tunnels carry the water under the Yellow River. About 330,000 people were resettled from the region of the expanded Danjiangkou Reservoir and from along the route of the canal. A "green belt" is being built along the entire route to reduce pollution from local industry and agriculture. There is also a tentative plan to move water from the Three Gorges Dam Reservoir by canal to the Danjiangkou Reservoir, to increase the flow northwards without undermining the industries and agriculture which depend on the water of the Han River.

• The *Western Route* will consist of three canals moving water from the headwaters of the Yangtze in the Qinghai-Tibetan Plateau and western Yunnan Plateau, to the headwaters of the Yellow River. Crossing the divide between these two watersheds in this mountainous region will be a huge engineering feat, which is still in the planning stage. When completed, these canals will transfer 17 cu. km of water to the Yellow River, expanding its flow to the Yellow Sea.

The Qinghai-Tibetan Plateau is known as *Sanjiangyuan*, i.e. "The Source of Three Rivers" (the Yangtze, the Yellow, and the Mekong). Also originating in southwestern China are the Brahmaputra and the Salween. Plans have been sketched out to transfer water to the North from the headwaters of the

The Danjiangkou Dam in Hubei Province.

The head of the middle route of the South-North Water Diversion Project.

The exit of the Qilihe Canal Inverted Siphon Project.

The Xiheishan flow division gate.

The Longquan Bridge in Shijiazhuang, capital city of Hebei Province.

The landscape bridge in Xingtai, Hebei Province.

three rivers which flow out from China—the Mekong, the Brahmaputra, and the Salween—which flow through India, Bangladesh, Myanmar, Laos, Thailand and Vietnam. But these are long-term plans at best, and would require agreement from the other nations. The completed Central Route is an engineering miracle—one of many miracles which are becoming common occurrences these days in China. Its water passes through tunnels dug under four rivers, and over the Caohe River Aqueduct in Henan Province, which is one of the "longest and most sophisticated ever built," according to a CCTV report. The water enters Beijing through a 9-km tunnel flowing 15 stories below ground, before finally being pumped into a new reservoir near the Summer Palace.

New Miracles in the Works

Two other projects are in the planning stages which can be considered part of the South-North transfer project. One is the Tianhe (Heavenly River) Project. Wang Guangqian, the president of Qinghai University and a member of the Chinese Academy of Sciences, is leading a team studying means of moving water in the atmospheric boundary layer and the troposphere, from above the headwaters of the Yangtze, north toward the headwaters of the Yellow River, and then provoking precipitation. The process is expected to move 5 cu. km of water into the North via the Yellow River annually.

A 45-minute video presentation titled "China's 'Heavenly River,' the Future of Water," by the LaRouche PAC science team, is available.

A second project is directed at the vast arid regions of the far west of China, in the Xinjiang Uyghur Autonomous Region. The idea is to build a series of tunnels and waterfalls, bringing water from the Qinghai-Tibetan Plateau to Xinjiang. The engineers working on the project call it the "Turning Xinjiang into

Wikimedia commons

Water tunnel of 600 km, under construction in Yunnan, is part of a pilot project to test technical capabilities to construct the Tibet-Xinjiang tunnel.

Yarlung Tsangpo River in Tibet (known as the "water tower of Asia"), through a series of tunnels and manmade waterfalls, to green part of the Taklamakan Desert in Xinjiang. The project would require large dams and pumping stations as well as tunnels, and would pose huge engineering challenges, as well as a huge cost. A water diversion project currently underway in Yunnan Province, which includes a 600 km tunnel, is seen as a demonstration project "to show we have the brains, muscle and tools to build super-long tunnels in hazardous terrain—and the cost doesn't break the bank," said Zhang Chuanqing at the Chinese Academy of Sciences' Institute of Rock and Soil Mechanics.

A plan for the Tibet-Xinjiang tunnel project was submitted to the central government in March 2017. A team of over 100 scientists did the planning.

California Project." Central California, once a desert, became America's breadbasket when the Central Valley Project, launched under Franklin Roosevelt in 1933, moved water from northern California to the San Joaquin Valley.

The proposed project would transfer water from the

Videos of the central route can be seen at: https://www.youtube.com/watch?v=7s5UungzXhw and https://www.youtube.com/watch?v=oBhAqvbcpqE&t=16s

china.org.cn

The Shunping section of China's South-North Water Diversion Project.

Now Govern, and Fix The Cape Town Water Crisis

by Ramasimong Phillip Tsokolibane

Feb. 19—No doubt there was celebration on the upper floors of office buildings in Wall Street and the City of London, and among sundry minions of His Royal Virus, Prince Phillip, and those of the whore of Babylon, that is, the decrepit Queen. With the help of their ass-kissing assets in our South Africa, and from deranged, re-arranged forces of U.S. ex-President Barack Obama and his mirror images and echoes in and around Washington, you have finally succeeded in removing our President, Jacob Zuma. There was dancing in aisles in the National Assembly, as only fools can

Residents of greater Cape Town queue to collect water from a spring.

dance, as the London-chosen Cyril Ramaphosa, was proclaimed South Africa's new President. We all know that for the most part, our Parliament is a place where political and other fools go to hide and play.

Jacob Zuma, however, despite what Cyril Ramaphosa, his fellow toadies and their faker media would have liked, did not shuffle off quietly into the sunset, but has vowed to remain an active fighter for those policies that have enabled South Africa to break out of the kraal of the British empire, policies that have thrust our

nation into the world and into a leadership position in the emerging new paradigm of peace and development coming from the East—President Xi's China, President Putin's Russia, and the BRICS alliance. Mr Zuma had asked that he remain in the Presidency until Summer, when South Africa will host the BRICS summit, but Mr Ramaphosa and his toadies in the ANC leadership said no. Mr Zuma deserved that honour, but he would not create more division and plunge the country toward a potential civil war by rendering the new government incapable of ruling.

Regardless of what the Brits believe about Mr Ramaphosa, he will find himself unable to reverse our nation's new historic march. If he tries, he has been forewarned that his Presidency will be stillborn.

So, we have a new government, and like all true South African patriots, I wish that government and, our new President, Mr Ramaphosa, well. I bid that it serve no interest but that of the South African people and discharge its constitutional duty to seek the best for all of our people, against any and all special interests or foreign adversaries.

What I say now does not contradict what I have said about the British-directed regime-change process that has brought Mr Ramaphosa to the Presidency. It is because of that ugly fact, that I—as the leader in this country of the international movement of American statesman and economist Lyndon LaRouche, whose efforts over the last half century, and those of his wife Helga, the 'Silk Road Lady,' have brought the world into the emerging New Paradigm,—that I must be the messenger of truth, giving an urgent message to our new President and his government: "You have demanded to step onto the stage and govern right now, so you must deal immediately and competently with the most urgent crisis facing our nation—the threat that the water will be turned off in June, if not earlier, for millions of our citizens in the Cape Town Metropolitan Municipality. This cannot be allowed to happen! To have a chance at averting this catastrophe, you will have to throw aside the narrow-minded thinking of Wall Street and London, the self-same people who have helped put you in power."

As I have stated before, we have not the time for finger-pointing and playing the blame game; there will be time enough to hold various people accountable for not taking the steps years ago that would have created new sources of fresh water to replenish that which has been depleted by predictable, cyclical drought. The problem has been the failure to adequately provide credit for such programs as desalination, on a massive scale, powered by safe nuclear energy, because various fools and bankers told us we could not. The monetarists think and talk about balancing books and spending only minimal amounts for such investment, and then expect to be paid back through hiked usage fees—policies which, in other cases, Mr Ramaphosa has proudly proclaimed as sound thinking. Now they balance their books and

expect debt repayment at terms that put our people at grave risk or even kill them, by wrongly thinking it is acceptable to just let the taps run dry in Cape Town.

As I wrote in my Feb. 6 statement, we must have a three-phased approach. In the short term, we must marshal all available resources, regionally, nationally, and internationally to bring adequate new fresh water into the system, at sufficient pressure to allow the taps to remain open. Let us call on our friends in Russia and China, as well as President Trump, to use temporarily the great nuclear-powered carriers of their navies, which have the capacity to desalinate large amounts of fresh water, while we look to other possibilities, in addition to the efforts already under way to bring new fresh water sources on line in Cape Town.

Let us simultaneously convene an emergency conference of the world's best minds on these matters, including from the nations mentioned, as well as the Israelis and the Spanish who are experts in creating fresh water sources, to discuss and determine what should be done. Let us quickly craft a workable plan and implement it.

Then let us devise a longer-term plan that will include credit provided by the BRICS' New Development Bank (NDB), whose Africa Regional Center is in Johannesburg, as well as the issuance of long-term fresh water development bonds by our national government. We must not listen to monetarists who say we can't do this, just because they do not want us to do it. It can be done when it comes to funding necessary infrastructure, as Mr LaRouche has long said.

All coordination, planning and construction must take place under the leadership of the President and the national government. That a declaration of disaster emergency was finally issued and the crisis "nationalised" recently was a positive step, one that should have taken place a long time ago.

Mr Ramaphosa has decided that he wants to be President right now. "Well, Mr Ramaphosa, you have inherited a deadly crisis and you must make this your first, and really only immediate priority. Your platitudes, of which you have uttered many in recent days, will simply not do."

I am prepared, as is my international organisation, to be of whatever help we can: "You wanted to lead, Mr Ramaphosa, so lead!"

mosimara@gmail.com

Hidden in Plain Sight

by R____'

1

It was an unseasonably warm late winter day. I was just returning from a visit to relatives in Dutchess County, and the ride down along the Hudson River was aburst with signs of new life and incipient spring. I was not able to enjoy any of these bounties which nature provides, however; rather, as I sat in the rail coach, my mind was in a state of extreme agitation, and my physical state was overwhelmed by a palpable involuntary tension and restlessness.

I consider myself to be a person who takes a serious interest in the affairs of our nation and, to the extent possible, those of the rest of the world as well. Yet, ti must be admitted here, that the recent inundation of stories in the news media, pertaining to the current controversies surrounding our President, is a subject to which I have not given the greatest scrutiny, and I have found much of the extreme political partisanship which seems to have come to characterize our culture extremely unpalatable.

It is perhaps this lack of attention, this apathy to exploring the nature of recent political happenings, which left me so thoroughly unprepared for the events which transpired during my just-concluded family visit.

Within what seems now to be only minutes upon arriving at my host's home, I learned—with some shock—of the extreme antagonism of my brother toward our President, expressed with a hostile vehemence that I would not earlier have thought possible. Then, over a span of not quite twenty-four hours, I was inundated with endless accusations and denunciations of the President's behavior, and these were accompanied by apparent evidence,—in the form of numerous news articles, statements from members of Congress, and editorials from prestigious publications—all of the form that the Executive of our nation has committed unprecedented crimes. Despite my initial aversion to pursuing the matter, my brother continued to thrust one piece of evidence after another before me, and although I would not have tolerated such aggressiveness from a stranger, I did not wish to disappoint a blood sibling with an appearance of disinterest in a matter that he held to such importance.

As the hours passed, I read, I listened, I examined, and throughout all of the experience my brother kept interjecting with phrases that contained words such as *treason* and *impeachment*.

I must confess; I did not hold up well during the course of this ordeal. Most shocking,—and the reality of this only gradually dawned on me—I found that as my departure neared, much of what my antagonist had argued, I now found to be sensible. I was—and am—not convinced as to the entirety of all of his utterances, but the evidence he presented seemed to be supported by the facts, and I am now deeply troubled as to the state of affairs in our nation's capital. Is it possible that a foreign nation committed an *act of war* against America by intervening into our election, as so many members of Congress have alleged? Have those close to the President lied under oath, perhaps at his behest? Are members of the President's family involved in criminal activity? The longer I pondered these and other accusations, the more unsettled I became, and the possibility arose that—Yes!—these allegations might, after all, all be true. But how was I to know for certain?

Such was my disordered mental condition during the lengthy return rail trip. As I disembarked at Grand Central Terminal, the sights and sounds of the metropolis barely registered on my psyche, and without consciously making a decision to do so, I found myself wandering along 42nd Street deep in thought, if one can term the anguished confusion gripping my mind as *thought*. At Bryant Park, the brilliant early crocuses grabbed my attention, but only fleetingly, and shortly I found myself standing in front of the Public Library. To enter, to go east, south, north, west—indecision and paralysis seemed to prevent any and all movement on my part.

2

I heard a voice call my name. "R____, R____, over here!" I turned, and there, only a dozen or so feet away stood my close friend M____. I call him a close friend, and indeed he has always struck me as a man of absolute integrity and remarkable intellectual insight, yet we had met only perhaps a half dozen times, and our total hours spent together could not possibly number more than twenty. For some reason a weight seemed to lift from off my spirit as he walked toward me.

He greeted me affably, with a warm smile, and we shook hands. "What are you doing here in mid-town?" he asked, knowing that I lived on the opposite shore of the East River. I explained that I had just arrived at Grand Central from an upstate trip, but as I tried to explain why I was currently standing in front of the Library, my speech was subverted by my mental agitation, and I stumbled over an explanation which seemed utterly incoherent even as I uttered the words.

M____ looked at me with what seemed to be a mixture of interest and bemusement. After a brief moment of silence, he said, "Look here, my friend, it is a beautiful day. Why don't we walk over to the park and you can tell me all about it?"

Within seconds we were moving. My friend led me over to the west side of Bryant Park, and soon we were seated on a bench near the statue of Benito Juárez.

"Tell me what is on your mind," he said.

Slowly, and then with increasing rapidness, all of the discussions of the last day tumbled from my lips. Much of it, admittedly, was disjointed, and in one sense my narrative resembled a series of eruptions with little coherence between the individual crisis points I attempted to describe. At the end, I stopped more out of mental exhaustion than through any sense of accomplishment of having told an intelligible narrative.

There then occurred a lull in our conversation which lasted at least a full sixty seconds. Finally, my friend spoke:

"There is much troubling in what you have said, but what concerns me more is your troubled state of mind. As to the issues you raise, I believe I can set your mind at ease, and if you agree to meet me tomorrow afternoon, I will provide you with material which should resolve all of your questions.

"There is, however, the matter of why you have fallen into such a deplorable condition. This, to me, is the greater issue. It bespeaks a weakness in your overall character, and a failure on your part to adequately develop the power that lies within your own mind. You are overwhelmed with masses of information—information which seemingly is factually true—but you have not discovered the means to process such *information*, to arrive at the truth when presented with an argument which seems convincing but is ultimately false.

"You have not yet learned to reason my friend; you are like Dante as he is just entering his fateful journey. I think I can help you, but I need to ponder these matters overnight."

I was taken aback at this response, but his compassion, more than his words, lifted my spirits; for, in truth the meaning of his counsel was so obscure that it seemed as if he had been addressing me in a foreign tongue. Nevertheless, we agreed to meet the next day at the front entrance to the Metropolitan Museum.

3

At home, in the evening, I pondered what my friend had said to me. In the hours since we had parted, my nervous condition had worsened, and the memory of his words seemed now to be mere gibberish. I found myself unable to sit still. Was I wrong about him? Was my faith in his good judgement misplaced? No! I knew him to be a trustworthy ally.

I sat in front of my computer and opened my e-mail program. Ten e-mails from my brother jumped off the screen. As I scanned them, I saw that they all contained links to a variety of articles. Almost mechanistically, I began opening the links.

One article reported that fifty-eight Democratic Congressmen had signed on to support Rep. Al Green's Bill of Impeachment against the President. Another quoted Congresswoman Maxine Waters calling the President despicable and a racist. Several articles quoted members of Congress, such as Jackie Speier and Eric Swalwell, charging that Russia had committed an Act of War against the United States, and they stated, or implied, that the President has committed treason by failing to respond to the Russian attack.

Other articles took up the investigations of Special Prosecutor Robert Mueller, an individual that most of the news media seem to hold in high regard. One reported that on Oct. 5, 2017, George Papadopoulos, described as a foreign policy advisor to the President, pled guilty to making false statements to FBI agents relating to contacts he had with agents of the Russian government. Another article, from Dec. 1, 2017, stated that the former national security adviser to the President, Michael Flynn, had pled guilty to lying to the FBI about conversations with Russia's ambassador. Yet another article said that, on Oct. 27, 2017, Paul Manafort, the President's campaign manager, had been indicted on charges of conspiring against the United States, money laundering, and acting as an unregistered agent of a foreign principal.

The final article reported on the Feb. 16, 2018 indictment, by Special Prosecutor Mueller, of thirteen Russians and three Russian companies for conspiring to interfere in the 2016 U.S. election.

My head was spinning. What was I to make of all of this? These were not diatribes from the gutter; all of these articles were published by respected institutions: the *New York Times*, the *Washington Post*, CNN, the *Guardian*, and others.

I telephoned my friend. He did not seem in the slightest surprised to hear from me at such a late hour. The thought occurred that he had been expecting this call, as if he could see my thoughts. I began to speak, and I got out a few sentences, but he interrupted: "Not tonight," he said. "It is late. Calm yourself. You are caught in a mental trap, and it is bedeviling you. All of this worry and anguish you are suffering will be removed tomorrow. We shall meet, and we shall resolve all of this."

I protested and attempted to continue, but he hushed me and repeated: "Tomorrow."

4

The next day, thirty minutes after the scheduled time for our rendezvous, M_____ was nowhere in sight. The steps of the Museum were awash with a boisterous crowd of people—perhaps there for some special exhibition—and I feared I had lost him in the crowd. An exhaustion overcame me, and it seemed as if I had slipped from my previous agitated state into one of uncaring melancholy.

Suddenly, he was at my side. "Forgive me, my friend, I was detained at a meeting inside, and this is the first I could break away." His presence immediately lifted my spirits, and when he suggested that we get away from the noise and hub-bub on the Museum steps, I readily acquiesced.

We rounded the side of the Museum and entered Central Park. Walking in silence for ten minutes, neither of us seemed prepared to address the problem at hand. At last, he stopped. "This is a good place here," he said. "Its sunny, and the grass is dry. Let's sit down and begin. Maybe our friend here will provide a guiding spirit." He gestured with his hand, and I looked to my left and saw, only a few feet off, a towering statue of Alexander Hamilton. Despite my apprehension, I was forced to smile, because my friend had spoken to me of Hamilton's greatness several times in the past.

"I have brought you," he began, "three documents. I would like you to read all three, today if possible. After you have done so, we can discuss the matters which so trouble you. There is no point in having such a conversation today, because your mind is filled with nonsense and misinformation."

From out of a small valise he took several papers and handed them to me. I read the three titles:

• *Robert Mueller Is an Amoral Legal Assassin: He Will Do His Job If You Let Him*
• *The Mueller Dossier Revisited: How the British and Obama Diddled the United States*
• *Mueller Indictments of Russian Social Media Trolls Scam the American People*

"These are all authored by the eminent Mrs. Barbara Boyd, an acquaintance of mine. Study carefully what she presents. I know you to be a serious thinker, in your own way, and an honest thorough examination of what is presented in these reports should answer all of the questions you have.

"However" he interjected, "I fear that, unless we have a different type of conversation, here and now, the deeper implications of what Mrs. Boyd has composed will be lost on you."

I was thoroughly mystified by the meaning of this last statement. I waited, but he clearly wanted me to say something. "Proceed," I blurted.

He took in a deep breath of air, exhaled, glanced up at the face of Hamilton, and began.

"Your problem, my dear R_____, is that you don't know how to think. No, No, please don't be insulted, for the malady you suffer from has become near universal in our day and age. You are afflicted with the illnesses of *deduction* and *induction*. These are forms of a mental disease, and they have become commonplace under the current dictatorship of *information*. Our people, sadly, have lost the ability to reason, and they think information—compiled bottom-up from dirty facts—represents the truth.

"Consider Pasteur's discovery in his work with tartaric acid, Beethoven's magnificent development of the Bachian Fugue, and Kepler's revolutionary insights into gravitation. Each of these was a discovery of something new, and each told us something truthful about our wondrous universe. These discoveries all violated accepted opinions—opinions based on facts that were believed in by the majority. True knowledge, the truth about anything, is never accomplished by starting with discrete facts and building up an amalgamation of evidence. One must begin with a universal idea, and test whether that idea, that hypothesis, is truthful.

"I can see, by your expression, that you are perplexed by what I am saying, but now I will say something which you shall probably find even more perplexing, and that is the following: If you wish to discover what is really going on with all of these attacks on the President, you must leave the realm of mathematical thinking."

To say that I was stunned and bewildered by his monologue would scarcely do justice to my reaction. His meaning was entirely beyond my comprehension. All I could manage was, "I am sorry, but I really don't follow what you are saying."

"I suspected as much, but all I am trying to do here is to plant a seed in your mind. Consider Euclid. He presents his theorems and proofs in the most logical way. One fact after another, building a mathematical lattice which seems unchallengeable. Yet, his system, like the fabled Tower of Babel, has a fatal flaw. All of his *proofs*, all of his logic are based on axioms, axioms which are taken on faith—beyond the worst fraud of the religious charlatan—and if you challenge and disprove one of his axioms, the whole edifice tumbles down.

"What you have read about the President, Robert Mueller, the Russians, and the rest all seems to present facts. But is that really all there is to this affair? Are there not underlying axiomatic aspects to this controversy that are not being discussed? Is there a different— a more truthful—narrative entirely than what Americans are spoon-fed in the news media?

"An obvious question to ask is *cui bono*, who benefits from this attempt to destroy the President? Motivation will begin to get you at the axiomatic issues involved."

Suddenly, he jumped up. "I am sorry; I must go. Read the documents. We must meet one more time. I will e-mail you with a location for tomorrow." And with that he was off.

I had not uttered a single word during any of this, nor when he strode off. His sudden departure was shocking and left me entirely unsettled. I didn't know what to think. Any movement seemed purposeless, for where would I go and what would I do? I looked at the documents he had left with me, lay down in the grass and began to read.

5

The next mid-day I made my way to the old Cooper Union, the site provided through an overnight email from M_____. The location seemed odd, for there was nothing within the range of visible sight that would appear to lend itself to the purpose of our meeting. This time I was tardy, and as I approached I saw that he had already arrived. We again exchanged greetings, and I asked, "Is this where we are meeting? There is nowhere to sit down."

"No," he said. "There is something that I would like you to see. Follow me."

He led me past the square and north on 4th Avenue. Our pace was moderate, and, as in the day before, no words passed between us as we progressed. Along the route, which continued for several blocks, here and there I spied a few buds on the trees, and the atmosphere seemed almost primaveral. Warmed by the bright sun, were it not for my impatience to continue our discourse, our ambulation would have been a thoroughly pleasant experience.

At 17th Street, my companion led me into the northern entrance to Union Square Park. There were couples and individuals occupying many of the table and chair arrangements, and we made our way around and through them, until M_____ stopped in front of the statue of Abraham Lincoln. He pointed up to the face of Lincoln and said, "This shall be our preamble. We will speak presently, but first … a moment…. Reflect on this man. Consider his mission. Ponder what drove him. A comprehension of Lincoln will begin to reveal the truth." His eyes were fixed upward as he uttered these words, and my gaze followed his.

He clapped me on the back and declared, "Come, let us find a place to sit." There were several empty tables in the immediate vicinity, but M_____ led me all the way down to the southern end of the park to where stood the equestrian statue of George Washington. He chose an empty table and we sat down.

"I chose this location," he began, "because the solution to your dilemma lies here. It will require seeing with more than just your eyes, but our present *environment* might spark the insight you seek.

"Now, answer me this: did you read the gifts I provided for you?"

"Yes. In fact, I went through them once in the afternoon, and then again, more attentively, late in evening."

"Good. What did you learn from them?"

I had been impatiently awaiting this opportunity to speak, but the wanderings up 4th Avenue and through the park had produced an effect such that, momentarily I was at a loss for words. "Well," I began, "as you know, I am not an especially *political* person, and there was so much information and so many individual people discussed who I am not familiar with, that it was all rather overwhelming."

"But surely," he prodded, "you must have reached some conclusions, or at the very least had some reaction to the contents. Start anywhere. Don't worry yourself about presenting a finished *analysis*. Just tell me what you think."

My lips tightened, my whole being seemed to compress into a coil, and I began:

"The first thing is that Robert Mueller seems to be a completely untrustworthy and un-reputable man." M_____ nodded. "His role in 9-11 and in the LaRouche case speaks volumes, and his actions in the investigation of the President seem motivated by an antagonism that, really, should suffice to disqualify him. Also, individuals within the intelligence community, such as James Comey and John Brennan appear to be fatally corrupted." I continued, "Then there is the thankless work done by Ray McGovern and William Binney. I don't claim to understand all of the specific technicalities, but it is clear that they have proven that the entire foundation for the investigation is false. Perhaps the most startling parts of the reports were those that dealt with Christopher Steele." Here, M_____ smiled. "All evidence points to him being an outright liar and trickster. Just based on the evidence of his lies alone, the case against the President seems to be a complete fabrication."

"So," M_____ replied, "you did study the reports. Good. Very good. Excellent. And did this effort satisfy you? Did it adequately refute all of charges that were pressed upon you during your visit upstate?"

"Yes, completely."

6

My friend seemed almost eerily calm. His hands were folded in his lap, and he was completely still, except for what seemed to be several, almost imperceptible, glances in the direction of Washington's statue.

Quietly, he began to speak: "You have made noteworthy progress, but I wonder if you discovered the tell-tale kernel of truth which is contained in what you have read, the one singularity which clarifies this whole affair. What you have presented so far can be represented thus: Your brother provided you with a series of facts. I presented another set of facts. You read both, you compared them, and you reached the conclusion that the reports I gave to you represented a more truthful rendition of these current affairs. This is good, as far as it goes, but it will not prevent you from making similar serious errors in the future. Your judgement is sound, but you are still operating in the realm of, at best, *inductive reasoning*. You take the facts as self-evident, and then you draw a conclusion from them.

"But there is something else to consider. There is one section, contained, within the reports, that you have not mentioned, and it is that content which redefines the entire species of what you are looking at. Do you know what it is?"

Involuntarily, I shook my head. "I am sorry but I cannot imagine what you are getting at."

Suddenly, animation gripped him: "Look around, my friend; look around, the answer is right here."

I glanced right and then left, but I said nothing, for all I saw where trees, tables, chairs and people conversing and eating.

M_____ pointed to the statue standing only feet away. "Do you know what that statue represents?" he asked.

"It is George Washington, on a horse."

"Yes, but do you know what *event* it depicts?"

I admitted I didn't.

"That is Washington, riding through the streets of Manhattan, on Nov. 25, 1783, the day that the British Army left New York. It is called Evacuation Day, the day of final triumph over the British Empire. Now! Let us finish this business! Do you remember, from your reading, the discussion of a man named Sir Richard Dearlove?"

"Yes, he was a British intelligence official, wasn't he?"

"Not merely any official. He was the head of MI-6, the British equivalent of the CIA. And do you recall the name Robert Hannigan?" I nodded. "He was the head of GCHQ, the British version of the National Security Agency. Do you remember what the reports say about those two men and their relationships with Christopher Steele?"

"They were both helping him, I believe."

"More than helping him. Sponsoring him, guiding him, manipulating all of his actions from the top. Dearlove has admitted that he advised Steele and aided in the creation of the notorious *dossier* upon which the entire investigation began. Think! This is the kernel which sheds light on the whole conspiracy. The entire tower of facts that have been used to accuse the President, facts now shown to be fraudulent, rests on a dossier created under the direction of high-echelon leaders of British Intelligence. And then it was Hannigan's GCHQ which passed these lies to the CIA in 2016. What this all shows is that the attack on the President originates from the highest level of the British establishment. And recall," he added, "this is not the first time Sir Dearlove has done this. As head of MI-6, he also was responsible for an earlier *dodgy dossier* which led to the second Iraq war.

"Do you begin to understand?" he asked. "Do you see that we are dealing with principles which define what the truth is?"

"So you are saying that it is the British who are behind all of this?" I asked. "I know I read the material, and I cannot argue with what is presented, but why would they do this?"

He gestured again at Washington's towering figure. "It is all here. It is right in front of you. Come, let us make our final stop."

He arose, and I followed him down the path, along the east side of the park. After one block we stopped, at yet another statue.

"Read to me the inscription which is printed here," he instructed.

The light was dim, but I read: *As soon as I heard of American independence, my heart was enlisted, 1776.* My eyes rose upward from the inscription, and I looked into the face of the Marquis de Lafayette.

"This statue," M_____ observed, "was sculpted by Frédéric-Auguste Bartholdi, the same individual who designed the Statue of Liberty."

We stood in silence. An inkling, a non-verbal provocation gripped me. A sense of unease—no, not unease, something else—more like an undefined idea, almost physical in its effect, seemed to be on the precipice of realization.

"My dear R_____, I must part from you now. My intention today is not to provide you with *answers*. If I have provoked you to pursue a method of investigation which will carry you to truthful insights, then I have succeeded. I wish you great joy in your efforts."

He grabbed my hand, clasped it firmly, spun, and was gone from sight within seconds, leaving me, in the company of our dear French hero, to consider all that had transpired.

The Foundations of Education's Destruction

by Mark Bender

The object of mankind is not to reproduce human individuals; the process of mankind is a higher one. It's the ability to generate and develop children who are geniuses in one degree or another; and therefore their existence becomes something sacred to all mankind—even when they're dead like he [Albert Einstein] was ... Because that value, that judgment, that insight into what the nature of mankind is; and mankind is not babies. Mankind is the creation of people, not babies.[1]

Increase Mather

Harvard College, 1726.

Prologue

In 1636, the Massachusetts Bay colony, barely seven years old and still struggling to feed itself, was already under attack by the British crown, in its effort to squelch this threat to imperial rule before it could spread further. In response, the colonial governing General Court voted—two full years before it established a militia for its defense—to establish the first university on American soil. In the next several years the Court enhanced this effort by creating a complete support structure for the young Harvard College, including public funding for schools, and laws requiring compulsory education for all youth in the colony.

As the imperialists continued to tighten their grip on the breakaway colony, one of the responses of the patriotic forces was to *increase* its defense of the educational institutions. The governing board of Harvard ultimately voted to install Increase Mather—a seasoned intelligence operative who had earlier founded the first Philosophical Society in the new world—as president in 1686. After the colony was placed under Royal rule in 1689, Harvard became the target of a full frontal assault by imperialist forces: members of the governing board were steadily evicted, finally culminating in the expulsion of Mather himself in 1701.

During its short 65 years as a truly independent institution of higher learning, Harvard can be said to have spawned a generation of revolutionary thinkers: many would continue in life as public figures, including, John Winthrop; John, Sam and John Quincy Adams; and John Hancock. It could be said that, without this institute of higher learning, there would not be a United States of America.

This lesson would not be lost on the British imperialists.[2]

---

1. Lyndon LaRouche, speaking to associates, Aug. 8, 2016. See https://larouchepac.com/20160815/einstein-standard-creative-progress

2. Lowry, Graham, *How the Nation was Won*, Executive Intelligence Review, 1988, p. 50.

by Howard Chandler Christy, 1940

The results of a moral education shown here by America's leaders during its formative years, at the signing of the U.S. Constitution.

Lost Cause?

America, today, is on the verge of losing the precious republic that our forefathers were willing to sacrifice their very lives to bring into being. Once a force to be envied around the world, our nation has become something that is feared, as we have now embraced the very imperial policies we once fought to free ourselves from. Yet, at the very time we are in desperate need of deliberation on the highest level, our internal discourse has been reduced to the level of squabbling *factions*—each one just as convinced of the rightness of its cause as the other—so determined to subdue the other that we have lost sight of our true enemy: the imperial forces that lie behind Wall Street, the financial front-men for the modern British oligarchy. How something which had been so clearly recognized by patriots of old as the source of power and influence behind the forces of global empire became accepted—yea, even respected—today is the story you are about to read. It is a story of corruption, but not in the simple sense of politicians taking money under the table. Yes, there will be copious amounts of money involved, but at the center is the corruption of your *mind*—not just *what* you think, but *how* you think—which would become the target.

To fully understand the motivation of what we will clearly come to see as a coordinated attack on one of the most fundamental institutions at the base of our republic—its entire education system—it is perhaps necessary to state that which was known to the nation's forefathers: at the base of our freedom stood independence—not in the way it is often understood today, in the liberal "I can do whatever I want" sense—but rather the independence of thought: the freedom to conceive a better condition for humanity as a whole, coupled with the freedom of action to bring that conception to fruition. If that sounds odd, you are beginning to see the roots of the problem. Simply put, our forefathers did not think as the majority of us do, today. For an Empire to continue to exist—a government which treats its subjects like animals—it needs those subjects to *conceive of themselves as animals*, to not possess any higher aspirations than simple personal survival, a place to eat, a place to work, and a place to sleep. The founding idea of our Republic—the conception that every child had the potential (whether realized or not) to advance the whole of mankind—is the ultimate threat to the survival of Empire. Just as the British came to understand that it was Christianity, with its conception of Man in the image of God—*imago viva Dei*—which was ultimately responsible for the "decline and fall" of the

Roman Empire, so too the British saw the growing *independence of thought* of America's youthful thinkers, with each one a potential genius, as one of the most significant threats to its continued ability to maintain and rule its extended empire. For that empire to survive, that view of humanity—of ourselves as instruments for its advancement and continuation—would have to be eliminated. It was us or them.

There are two complementary themes which will run side by side through our story, first that of the growth in power and influence of private "philanthropical" foundations and the vast hoards of cash at the disposal of private, non-elected (and thus unaccountable) individuals, and second, of their primary and continuing target, the take-over and take-down of the nation's education system. The ultimate benefactor of this attack would be the forces of finance—"Wall Street," the money changers within the temple—front men for the imperial forces against which we fought for our Independence nearly 250 years ago. If this sounds like ancient history, stop and ask yourself: "Why?" Because if we are going to rid ourselves of this pestilence, and finally secure for ourselves the "blessings of Liberty" for our children, joining the rest of the world in moving humanity forward, we must regain that understanding.

The specific strategy of the British, then, was to enforce an artificial limit on our thinking—their unaware victims—to eliminate just that most elevated aspect of human thought from which universal concepts such Life, Liberty, and the Pursuit of Happiness spring and are understood. As later formulated by the 20th Century British operative Lord Bertrand Russell, the ultimate intent of the education system was to induce in the student the "unshakable conviction that snow is black." First, students were to be taught that their place in the world was no higher than that of a manual laborer, and eventually no better than an animal. Then, the entire concept of "knowledge" as a universal concept would be torn asunder. No more would we be allowed to entertain any notions of Natural Law at the heart of the European Renaissance, or that the world is governed by universal truths, or that knowledge of such is attainable by mankind. In its place we will see the introduction of a "segregated" concept of reality, one more amenable to the goals of the oligarchy, through the growth of the newly invented "social" studies: Lord Russell himself championed the newly elevated reductionist discipline of mathematics, and its epistemological cousin, statistics. This, combined with a socially generated conformity—an induced fear within the individual of not wanting to be perceived as being "different"—all contributed to subdue that aspect of human nature from whence true genius springs.

Target Education

Philanthropy, the use of one's *private* fortune, distributed ostensibly for the *public* good, is indeed a noble-sounding idea. Who could argue with the person who seeks to give back to the very social order which has served as the source for their original enrichment? Doesn't one in fact actually "owe" something to that (our) society, and shouldn't we allow—nay, even encourage such behavior? After all, "You can't take it with you," right? All this ignores the corrupting effect of money for money's sake, and, as we shall see, the motivation and goals of the individual, corrupted by wealth, may, and in fact are almost guaranteed to run counter to those of society at large. Although this aspect of empire gets almost no explicit discussion among the early American writers, this was understood to be one of the aspects of Old European society—with its fixed, stratified class structure of permanently rich and permanently poor—which the original colonists were determined to prevent from emerging on American soil. Private fortunes, known as *fondi*, are the subject of much literature and their demise was thus "in the blood" of revolutionary freedom-minded thinkers of the colonial era. If we are to win this battle, they must again become the target.

Of all the constitutional institutions which the founders left us to preserve our precious republic, the education system—upon which the other institutions would ultimately stand or fall—was so basic, it was not even considered necessary to mention in the original documents. In fact, the federal Department of Education only became established in 1969, and acts as more of an enforcer of the status quo than an innovator. In today's factionalized political environment, the current debate over chartered (private, for profit) schools has become muddled, with the "profit motive" obscuring the larger reality that, through privatization, we are effectively putting control of the minds of our children in the hands of this treasonous entity, Wall Street. The fact is that this current debate is just the culmination of a long struggle—most of which we (patriots) have ultimately lost—going back over 150 years. The success of the forces of finance in this very public takeover has been partly due to the fact that, while so many understand the threat of "big banks" and corporate money, it has been the soft cop of "philanthropic" institutions—essentially privatized corporate profits—which has been behind the takeover of our schools.

Through the first century of our nation's development, the institutions of higher learning were almost universally in the hands of religious institutions, which ran universities as an extension of their seminaries, training an educated secular elite along side the religious leadership. Education was thus seen as a *moral* institution, with the study of the Greek and Latin classics of Plato and Cicero on equal footing with the Holy Scriptures. There were no "subjects"—mathematics, economics or (especially) social studies—in this curriculum. Knowledge was understood to be universal, as was the mind's ability to comprehend it. Through this American system of education were thus created some of the finest *universal* thinkers of the times, individuals who saw the existence of Empire as being antithetical to humanity's very nature as a creative species, a parasite which reduced its victims to mere "subjects," by robbing them of the freedom and depth of thought necessary for the development of humanity as a whole.

By the time of the Revolution, the colonies supported numerous major institutions, each connected to any of several religious sects, in keeping with our belief in freedom of religion. Uniquely, through the efforts of George Washington, "King's College" was eventually chartered in the heart of New York City (changing its name to Columbia University shortly after the success of the Revolution). Although originally identified with the Anglicans, Columbia thus became the first distinctly non-sectarian (and thus uniquely "independent") university in the newly created nation. As evidence of the genius produced in those early days, we have only to view its website, where we are immediately reminded that, "Among the earliest students and trustees of King's College were John Jay, the first chief justice of the United States; Alexander Hamilton, the first secretary

Library of Congress

General Robert E. Lee (seated, in light suit) surrendering to General Ulysses S. Grant at Appomattox, April 9, 1865. After the British lost any chance of militarily regaining their former colonies, they turned to subverting education in the U.S. Republic.

of the treasury; Gouverneur Morris, the author of the final draft of the U.S. Constitution; and Robert R. Livingston, a member of the five-man committee that drafted the Declaration of Independence."

It was in the days following the surrender of Confederate General Robert E. Lee at Appomattox, in the summer of 1865, that the operation to subvert the education institutions of America went into high gear. That war was the failed last hope of the British to see the fledgling former American colonies subdued militarily. With the military option now finally eliminated, the British turned to other means of subversion.

London Calling

It is here that our story takes a decided turn, for, in 1867, we find the aged financier George Peabody, ill of health and eager to salve his ailing soul, depositing the otherwise overly generous sum of $1,000,000 with the board of trustees of his newly created "philanthropic" instrument, the Peabody Education Fund (PEF). Launched with a board of directors studded with luminaries, including war heroes General Ulysses S. Grant and Admiral David G. Farragut, also present on the board was "the President's banker," George Washington Riggs. Mr. Peabody's money was to be distributed by this august board, which eventually included Mr.

John Pierpont Morgan himself, "to aid the stricken south" through scholarships and grants for schools.

George Peabody, a Baltimore native, had early partnered with Mr. Riggs in a dry goods distributorship, Peabody & Riggs, and made a fortune. Then in 1832, Peabody decided to *repatriate* to the mother country, moving to London where he spent—outside of returning for two auspiciously timed "tours" of the South, the first in 1857 and again 1866—the remainder of his life. Peabody eventually became a partner with Junius Spenser Morgan (J.P.'s father)—founding with him the bank which would eventually become the imposing Wall Street firm, the House of Morgan—and was so close to the Queen that she had given him a portrait of herself and had a statue of this prodigal subject raised in the financial district of London.[3]

Between 1865 and 1876, under both Reconstruction state governments and the Grant Presidency, revolutionary progress had been accomplished in education in the South, including that region's first system of universal public education, as well as the establishment of numerous colleges and institutions of higher learning. This development—to educate both the former slaves and the poor whites—was bitterly opposed by the oligarchical elite, in both the North and South, and by 1875-1876 it was under all-out assault.

In 1875, Peabody's Education Fund finally succeeded in opening the first "normal" school designed to train teachers in the monarchy-approved "man as mere laborer" de-education program. Not that the financial frontmen hadn't wanted to do this earlier. It just took them that long—with three failed attempts, beginning in 1868—to get the Tennessee state legislature to approve the funds, which only finally happened after the Peabody board threatened to close up shop and take all

George Peabody

of their money to Georgia. So controversial was this school—originally named the State Normal School, it underwent three name changes in the next 50 years—that it had to be set on "neutral" land of the former Nashville State University, itself recently renamed Vanderbilt University after a $1,000,000 gift from Yankee railroader (then the richest man in America), "Commodore" Cornelius Vanderbilt.[4]

Far from being appreciative subjects and just accepting this noble gesture, what the Tennessee lawmakers had repeatedly balked at was the idea that the state should fund something over which it would have no control—specifically that this private Peabody Fund (soon to be known as a "foundation") was demanding total autonomy over the public curriculum. That these fears were in fact justified, we have the words of Dr. Ernest Victor Hollis, writing in his 1938 *Philanthropic Foundations and Higher Education*, "During the next five years [1875-1880]," Hollis wrote, "the Nashville experiment was a crucible in which was tested almost every phase of [philanthropic] foundation relationship to state higher education."[5]

This issue, of the method of education appropriate for Mankind as a creative species, and not confined to manual labor, was addressed directly by perhaps the greatest thinker of the day, W.E.B. DuBois, in his 1903 book, *The Souls of Black Folk*. Reflecting on this philosophical argument, DuBois made the point clear, as he

---

3. Curry, J.L.M., *A Brief Sketch of George Peabody and a History of the Peabody Education Fund through thirty years* (Cambridge University Press: John Wilson and Son, 1898), p. 23.

4. In 1905, when the then-named Peabody Education College for Teachers separated from Vanderbilt, it sought the land on which was situated the Roger Williams University, one of four colleges founded in Nashville for freed slaves. Begun in 1864 as Bible classes in the home of Daniel W. Phillips, a white Baptist minister from Massachusetts, but which had blacks on the board, it was, most notably, not part with the foundation "program." When the Roger Williams University refused to sell their property, two separate fires suspiciously occurred there, which succeeded in shutting the University down, and eventually forcing them to sell their property to the Peabody institution.

5. Hollis, Ernest Victor, PhD. *Philanthropic Foundations and Higher Education*, Columbia University Press, 1938, p. 34.

wrote, "The tendency is here, born of slavery and quickened to renewed life by the crazy imperialism of the day, to regard human beings as among the material resources of a land to be trained with an eye single to future dividends …. [W]e daily hear that an education that encourages aspiration, that sets the loftiest ideals and seeks as an end culture and character rather than bread-winning is the privilege of white men and the danger and delusion of the black."[6] DuBois continued his fight on this principle, which eventually became a central issue in the foundation of the National Association for the Advancement of Colored People, in 1909.

It is to be noted here that Mr. Peabody, the ostensible source of the privatized money involved, is dead, or soon would be. You would be fully justified, then, if you were to ask just exactly who, or what we are talking about, when we identify the funds distributed through the vehicle of the Peabody Education Fund. The funds were placed in the hands of a board of directors, upon which (as we saw) sat Mr. J.P. Morgan, then the most formidable name in finance, with the full weight of the British monarchy behind him. Not willing to confine themselves to the day to day work that the supervision of this pile of money would require, Mr. Morgan and the board selected an agent, in this case the Reverend Doctor Barnas Sears, to do that work for them. Mr. Sears was considered a "Reverend" having been ordained by the First Baptist Church, and a "Doctor," for having been President of Brown University, up to the point at which his newfound devotion to this cause led him to leave the comfort of his native Boston home, and take up residence in the bucolic town of Staunton, Virginia.

Perhaps the Reverend Doctor saw himself in the image of the renegade crusader, Martin Luther, having authored, in 1849, a book, *The Life of Luther: With Special Reference To Its Earlier Periods And The Opening Scenes Of the Reformation,* with noted emphasis, and possible parallels, on his early life. Or perhaps he had recommended himself in an earlier post he held from 1855-1861, as one of the nation's first Secretaries of Education, that in the state of Massachusetts. Shortly after he had assumed the position of agent for the Peabody Education Board, a letter Mr. Sears wrote was then deemed "fit to print" by the *New York Times.* Written to a fund recipient in Louisiana, and appearing in print on May 22, 1867, it well describes his (and the board's) intent:

Hon. R. M. Lusher:

DEAR SIR—Nothing that has reached me from the various Southern States has given me such unmingled satisfaction as the perusal of your report, just received. It is, in most respects, just such a document as the Trustees of the Peabody Educational Fund, in like circumstances, would have written…

We propose to limit our aid to such modes as shall tend to the establishment of a system of public schools. We desire that the whole system and its administration be in the hands of the people. The only conditions that we shall insist on will be that the schools shall be, or tend to become, public free schools. By "free schools" I do not mean schools equally open to whites and blacks. All such matters we propose to leave to the people themselves.

We wish to act exclusively through school organizations in existence among the people, and to have no schools of our own. We do not

photographic print by C.M. Battey, 1918, Library of Congress

W.E.B. DuBois

SOULS OF BLACK FOLK

ESSAYS AND SKETCHES

BY

W. E. BURGHARDT DU BOIS

SECOND EDITION

CHICAGO
A. C. McCLURG & CO.
1903

---

6. DuBois, W. E. B., *The Souls of Black Folk* (McClurg & Co., Chicago, 1903). Chapter III. Downloadable at: http://www.bartleby.com/114/

desire to own schoolhouses, to employ teachers, nor to superintend schools. This would devolve too much labor and expense, and, what is still worse, would be introducing a foreign element which would work badly in every respect.

I intend to visit your State next Winter, when I shall desire very much to see you, and confer with you about the best way of distributing our aid. The inclosed circular will show that our policy will be to cooperate, as far as possible, with State and municipal authorities.

To say a word of your system—it appears to be best and most congenial to our forms of government to have the schools supported, in part, from a State fund, but chiefly by local taxation. Municipalities always administer funds raised by themselves better than those that belong to the State.

The people bear a local tax imposed by themselves for their own benefit much more patiently than a State tax for the schools of the State generally. So, at least, I have found it, as far as my observation has extended. But a State School Fund is necessary *in order to attach the cities and townships to the State system*; for the benefits of the fund can be limited to those who fulfil all the conditions imposed by the State...[7] (emphasis added)

The program of the Peabody Education Board then, was to spread around some monarchy-approved millions of dollars, in the vast wasteland spawned by a British-promoted Civil War amongst her lost colonies, to *determine the direction* of Southern education, while all the time promoting the utilitarian program of manual, industrial instruction. But, we were not to be concerned, because Mr. Peabody's fund was "race neutral," eager

Freedmen's Bureau office in Memphis, Tennessee, 1866.

to support either "separate" or "mixed" schools. For the Fund and the British financial monarchy behind it, it was the program which was important.

Peabody, who, upon his death in 1869, doubled his philanthropic contribution to $2 million,[8] would, in 1882, be joined in this subversive task by Connecticut textile merchant and Congregational Church evangelist John F. Slater, with his newly established Slater Fund for the Education of Freedmen. Slater, who poured an additional $2 million into the cause, earned recognition for his work in the form of "a vote of thanks and a medal" from the U.S. Congress. While these several millions of privatized, foundation money, sown on the desolate fields of the ruined South, were still small compared to the estimated $16 million spent by the federal Freedmen's Bureau, that number was about to change, in a very big way.

Wall Street Takes Over

In 1901, Robert Ogden, newly rich from his portion of the Philadelphia-based Wanamaker Department Store fortune, chartered a train on which several dozens of the country's richest citizens were conveyed through-

---

7. Sears, Barnas, The Peabody Fund—Letter, dated May 22, in *New York Times*, June 8, 1867, ProQuest Historical Newspapers The New York Times (1851-2011).

8. In 1911, when the Peabody Education Fund dissolved, their remaining $1,300,000.00 went to the Peabody Education College for Teachers, in Nashville, Tennessee.

out the still-unrecovered South, their sojourn eventually terminating in Athens, Georgia, where Mr. Ogden had arranged that a Conference on Southern Education would take place. In what John D. Rockefeller, Jr. later recalled as "one of the outstanding events of my life," this erstwhile crew was otherwise dubbed "Pullman car philanthropy," in light of its object.

That same year, J.P. Morgan, still the leading PEF trustee, wrested control of the Carnegie Steel Company from its founder and owner, Andrew Carnegie, paying the then astounding sum of $500,000,000, and finally breaking the spirit of this once great industrialist. The buyout of his company was the final blow to Carnegie, a man who had stood against Wall Street policies for most of his life, producing a necessary product for the nation's growth while paying his workers a living wage and otherwise caring for their welfare. From this point on, the Carnegie name, which had lent itself to the construction of numerous libraries and other buildings on college campuses across America, would be used against itself, lending cover of his good name to projects now destructive of the national interest. Together with oil magnate John D. Rockefeller, Sr., this combination of Morgan-corrupted and Morgan-made multi-millionaires represented the next pincer move in the destruction of our education system.

In 1902, in conjunction with the Atlanta conference, the senior Rockefeller inaugurated what he dubbed the General Education Board—fully in support of the utilitarian program initially advocated by the Peabody

Library of Congress

J.P. Morgan

Education Fund—with a $1,000,000 donation. A direct continuation of the PEF, the new Board absorbed in the process many of its functions, as well as members themselves. The Board also received an official charter from Congress, signed by newly inaugurated anglophile imperialist President Teddy Roosevelt on Jan. 12, 1903. On top of the effect on education of the country's youth, what we begin to see is literally the formation of a new layer of society, through the ever increasing interlock of directors (especially between foundations and universities, along with corporate boards), and the increasing numbers of middlemen—who came to be called the "philanthropoids"—between the (donor's) money and the (recipient) client. A detailed description of board members of the General Education Board (GEB) and their affiliations will serve to illustrate the point:

Before 1902 the eleven original trustees of this Board had directed four separate educational philanthropies: the American Baptist Education Society (ABES), the Peabody Education Fund, the Slater Fund, and the Southern Education Board. J.L.M. Curry and Wallace Buttrick were executive directors of the Peabody and Slater funds; Walter Hines Page and Albert Shaw were editors of national repute and were seasoned foundation trustees. Robert C. Ogden and George Foster Peabody [son] were merchants of an order comparable to John Wanamaker and Marshall Field and,

Library of Congress

Andrew Carnegie

through the Southern Education Board, each of them had been a personal crusader for improved educational conditions in the South. Daniel C. Gilman brought to the Board the qualities that made Johns Hopkins a great university, and also his experience as a trustee of the Slater Fund. Morris K. Jesup was a [J.P. Morgan-connected] financier and a philanthropist with sound experience as a foundation trustee; William H. Baldwin, Jr., was a corporation lawyer and Slater trustee. Frederick T. Gates, the elder Rockefeller's mentor in his earlier giving, and John D. Rockefeller, Jr ... were on the original board.[9]

John Fox Slater

The nominal leaders of foundations and of leading universities begin to slide back and forth, exchanging positions so easily as if to drive home the point that the control of the nation's education system was now firmly in the hands of Wall Street.

At the dawn of the Twentieth Century, John D, Rockefeller, Sr. had so much money that it was literally making him sick; requests for his fortune were thus nagging at his soul. A devout Baptist, who firmly believed that his ability to make money "came from God," Rockefeller soon came to trust one Reverend Frederick T. Gates—whom he had encountered in his earliest days of philanthropy, through the American Baptist Education Society—with the management (distribution) of his funds. Gates, a fellow Baptist (who had been ordained a minister in 1880) had become the Corresponding Secretary of the ABES, which had been established in conjunction with the Rockefeller financing of the University of Chicago, a project which J.D. Rockefeller, Sr. seeded with over $600,000, beginning in 1890. After first easing the conscience (distributing the funds) of minor millionaire Charles Alfred Pillsbury, in 1889, Gates (apparently deciding he wanted to get "closer to God") left the ministry and went to work directly for Rockefeller.

While Rockefeller's money thus targeted the nation's primary education infrastructure (only later branching out to high schools and colleges), the Carnegie name, drawing on its former goodwill, was used to lead Wall Street's frontal attack on the nation's secondary education system. In 1905, Carnegie would throw a hand grenade into the mix, by launching the "Fund for Aged University and Technical School Teachers," and endowing it with a $10,000,000 donation. This otherwise magnanimous contribution, to ostensibly provide pensions for retiring professors, was, however, a mere "carrot" in the effort of "reform" of the nation's secondary education system. The "hook," in the form of qualifying clauses, shook the system to the core. Mr. Carnegie's own words were quoted in an incredulous *New York Times*: "Only such as are under control of a [religious] sect or require trustees, officers, faculty, or students, to belong to any specified sect, or which impose any theological test, are to be excluded." In other words, in order to qualify for payouts, venerated universities would have to undergo a "forced secularization" in the form of segregating themselves from any sort of ties to religious institutions, their financing, or oversight. Carnegie's money easily recruited 21 professors to the board of his fund (which totalled 25), including Presidents A.T. Hadley of Yale; Charles W. Eliot of Harvard; William R. Harper of the University of Chicago; Nicholas Murray Butler of New York's Columbia University; and Woodrow Wilson of Princeton.[10]

Effectively recruiting the entire teaching force of the nation's universities as allies—and in the process transforming many honest intellectuals into money-chasing, *brotgelehrte* academics—Carnegie's financial carrot forced a top-down shakeout of the nation's education institutions, furthering the oligarchical quest to gain control of the institutions of higher learning. Colleges were forced to open their books (financial as well

---

9. *Ibid*, Hollis, p. 91.

10. Entire board listed in "Carnegie Millions for Pension Fund," *New York Times*, April 28, 1905, ProQuest Historical Newspapers, New York Times (1851-2011), p. 1.

as classroom), to reveal any hidden sources of financial support, with Carnegie's Fund going so far as to issue a Bulletin Number 3 to provide "Standard Forms for Financial Reports of Colleges, Universities, and Technical Schools" to ensure full compliance.[11] No longer would they be allowed to be governed by a body led by church elders, nor would they have a veto over the new "progressive" course structure. Carnegie men (primarily accountants) who soon blanketed the country, became derogatorily known as "standardizers," one of their major accomplishments being the installation of the now-ubiquitous college "credit," further imposing a uniform structure on the institutions.

This forced "liberalizing" of the course structure—creating, as if overnight, the specialized disciplines of economics, anthropology, history and psychology (among others)—thus accomplished with privatized money, included the forced ascendance of mathematics over physics in the science world, coinciding with the efforts of Lord Bertrand Russell, who first came to the United States in 1905. Here we would see the rise of the newly invented "social" sciences, where a new form of empirical, now christened "scientific," inquiry was being developed, involving the application of (mathematical) statistical methods to social problems and relationships. This became fertile ground for development of concepts such as the Bell Curve (eventually popularized in the 1960s), where any sample grouping is compressed into a mathematical formula, reducing life to some combination of means, averages and standard deviations. All who don't fit into the curve are either

Wikimedia Commons

John D. Rockefeller

forced into it, or, if their conscience or their creativity won't let them conform, they will literally be deemed unfit and condemned as a pariah of society.[12]

This was too much, even for the normally finance-defending *Wall Street Journal*, which, on April 28, 1905, published an editorial, "Breadth that is Narrowness," charging that "He provided that such colleges as are under control of a sect … or which imposes any theological test, are to be excluded … There is, therefore, a certain narrowness to Mr. Carnegie's philanthropy which limits the scope of its beneficent purpose … *they have largely sacrificed intensity of conviction* for so-called 'breadth of view.'" Appended to this was a note of an uncorrupted college instructor: "When we enter the teaching profession we do not do it with the expectation of making money; we have an entirely different end in view. This pension system would certainly lower our standard."[13] (emphasis added)

Another fierce critic of the time was a young investigative journalist (they were derogatively referred to as "muckrakers" in that day) by the name of Upton Sinclair, who toured the country shortly after World War I, finally producing a stinging critique of education he titled—just as the world was coming to fear Benito Mussolini and fascism—*The Goose Step*. Sinclair's book, which he was forced to self-publish in 1923 after being rejected by every "establishment" publisher in the nation, provided an exhaustive profile of what the

---

11. Referenced in *A Handbook of the Public Benefactions of Andrew Carnegie*, The Rumford Press, Concord, N.H., 1919, p 34. A total of 16 bulletins were printed between 1907 and 1922. The entire set is view/downloadable here: https://catalog.hathitrust.org/Record/006179510

12. For a detailed discussion of the implications of the prioritizing of mathematics over physics, see "Hilbert and Russell, the Suffocation of Science by Mathematics," by Phil Rubenstein, *Executive Intelligence Review*, June 12, 2015. Beginning in the 1970s we will have ritalin to make this "conforming" less difficult.

13. "Breadth That Is Narrowness," *Wall Street Journal*, April 28, 1905. ProQuest Historical Newspapers The Wall Street Journal (1889-1997), p. 1.

leadership of leading universities was to become under the influence of Wall Street money, demonstrating, in the process, just how thoroughly the nation's education institutions had been corrupted by the financiers. Sinclair saved perhaps his most vicious criticism for Columbia University, which he dubbed "The University of the House of Morgan." Writing of Columbia's then-president, Nicholas Murray Butler, Sinclair declares, "Butler considers himself the intellectual leader of the American plutocracy; he takes that role quite frankly, and enacts it with grave solemnity... There has never been a more complete Tory in our public life; to him there is no 'people,' there is only 'the mob,' and he never wearies of thundering against it."[14]

With its reach steadily extending beyond elementary education, by 1921, J.D. Rockefeller, Sr. (who would live to be a sad 98 years of age, dying in 1937) had sown an astounding total of $128,000,000 into the primary education system, through his General Education Board. Carnegie had contributed additional millions,[15] although his money would be spread to internationalist institutions as well, with his Endowment for International Peace appearing in 1913, just as the world was to become engulfed in its first World War. At this point, we find the "magnanimous" philanthropic contributions drop from the headlines—partly because the financial oligarchy actually prefers to work in the shadows—with the ostensible explanation being the hostilities involved in the war. The reality is that they were about to encounter the instinctive patriotic backlash to the diktat by excessive wealth, this in the form of the Walsh Commission.

American Backlash

Officially established in 1912, the Commission on Industrial Relations spent two full years—across two separate Congresses and administrations—investigating labor abuses nationwide. Its final report filed 11 volumes of written and oral testimony. While not initially centered on philanthropic foundations (or education), it eventually investigated large concentrations of "economic power" and the "interlocking directories," specifically of the Rockefeller and Carnegie funds, and ultimately it delivered a setback to the onslaught of privatized corporate money upon the country. The popular argument was that this money was somehow "tainted" because of the implication that it was gotten through exploitation of the workers involved (i.e. excessive profits from low wages and long hours).

The investigation came to be known as the Walsh Commission, after its head, Kansas City labor lawyer Frank Walsh, a fiery Irishman who reportedly once told a friend that, "I hate like hell to be respectable," adding that, "what we need more than lawmakers and law governors is agitators. An agitator is a man who won't stand for lies [just] because they are told." In 1915, Walsh famously grilled John D. Rockefeller, Jr on the witness stand for three days running. Walsh's immediate focus was one of the most serious "abuses" of labor which had occurred in this country up to that time: the April 20, 1914 Ludlow Massacre on Easter Sunday evening, in which Rockefeller-hired goons and Colorado National Guardsmen had attacked a camp of striking miners and their families at the Rockefeller-owned Colorado Fuel & Iron Corporation, killing between 19 and 26, including 2 women and 11 children.

The Commission, spanning as it did the Presidencies of first William Howard Taft, then Woodrow Wilson, was so contentious that the nine member board actually produced three separate final reports.[16] The issue of subversion by the philanthropic foundations was directly addressed in testimony of future Supreme Court Justice Louis D. Brandeis, on Jan. 23, 1915:

> ...when you have created a great power, when there exist these powerful organizations who can afford—not only can successfully summon forces from all parts of the country—but can afford to use tremendous amounts of money in any conflict to carry out what they deem to be their business principle, and can also afford to suffer losses—you have necessarily a condition of inequality between the two contending

14. Sinclair, Upton, *The Goose Step: A Study of American Education* (Pasadena, California: Published by the Author, 1923).

15. Then, ten years later, the object attained, he took it all back. "Several studies of pensions were initiated by the Foundation," writes Hollis, "and in 1915 President [Henry] Pritchett [formerly President of MIT] announced what amounted to a repudiation of the Foundation's initial philosophy of pensions. The new philosophy declared that free pensions were harmful to the beneficiaries, could not be financed by the Foundation, and were not fair to the great majority of college teachers outside the affiliated institutions." (See note 5, p. 192.) In reality, Carnegie's funds went to a very narrow group of universities, ones chosen to be the leaders in national education reform.

16. Ultimately, over 110,000 copies of the final report were printed, 10,000 bound in cloth, by order of the Commission.

forces.... In the cases of these large corporations the result has been to develop a benevolent absolutism—an absolutism all the same; and it is that which makes the great corporation so dangerous. It is because you have created within the State a state so powerful that the ordinary social and industrial forces existing are insufficient to cope with it.[17]

The Commission recommended that Congress "enact legislation limiting the amount of funds and the exercise of power by fund managers." Provisions against accumulation of unexpended income and against expenditure in any year of more than 10% of capital were demanded, together with rigid inspection of finances (investment and expenditure) and complete publicity through open reports to the government. In addition, the report proposed the creation of an investigatory body for the continued study of activities of foundations and called for increased "government activity in education and the social services to balance the power of foundations." In other words, had Congress acted at this point to curb the growing but not yet pervasive influence of private foundations, it could have defeated this flanking operation of the enemy.

While the Commission put up a strong fight, it was clear it did not comprehend the threat posed by this new foe. In 1910, and continuing throughout these proceedings, Rockefeller chose to try to obtain a federal charter for an official Rockefeller Foundation (the one in existence today, separate from the General Education Board). But his demands were such—most egregious was that he wanted existing federal laws against perpetuities ignored or repealed—that Congress could not bring themselves to pass it, voting the charter down three times, flat. After three years of trying, Rockefeller then shifted gears, and simply went to the State of New

University of Chicago Archives
Fredrick T. Gates, circa *1890.*

York, where, with the threat that he might take his billions elsewhere, he "promptly secured from the New York State legislature what Congress refused to grant. The Sage and Carnegie foundations did the same." In the words of Hollis, "This ought not to be possible."[18]

'Whatever It Costs'

After being effectively set back for several years, the Anglophile American oligarchy was about to come back with a vengeance. In 1916, just as our nation was in the process of being dragged into its first geopolitical war in Old Europe, the Morgan/Rockefeller GEB issued two of what it dubbed "occasional" policy papers, through which the Board shed its benevolent cloak and declared its full oligarchical intentions. The first, *The Country School of Tomorrow,* written by the money-corrupted Frederick Gates, although set as a fictionalized "dream," declared the ultimate goal of these Wall Street agents: nothing less than the complete destruction of the nation's (intellectual) independence. Here are the words of Gates:

In our dream, we have limitless resources and the people yield themselves with perfect docility to our molding hand. The present educational conventions fade from their minds; and, unhampered by tradition, we work our own good will upon a grateful and responsive rural folk. *We shall not try to make these people or any of their children into philosophers or men of learning, or men of science. We have not to raise up from among them authors, editors, poets or men of letters. We shall not search for embryo great artists, painters, musicians. Nor will we cherish even the humbler ambition to raise up from among them lawyers, doctors, preachers, politicians, statesmen, of whom we now have ample supply....*

The task we set before ourselves is very

<hr>

17. House Commission on Industrial Relations, Hearings, Final Report, Barnard & Miller Print, Chicago, 1915, pp. 82-83. https://archive.org/stream/finalreportofcom00unitiala#page/82/mode/2up

18. *Ibid,* Hollis, p. 7.

simple as well as a very beautiful one, to train these people as we find them to a perfectly ideal life *just where they are.*

So we will organize our children into a little community and teach them to do in a perfect way the things their fathers and mothers are doing in an imperfect way, in the homes, in the shops and on the farm.[19]

Occasional Paper #2 featured a work by Board member and Harvard President Charles William Eliot, "Changes Needed in American Secondary Education." Eliot, a relative of the famed naturalist poet, and at the time the youngest and longest-serving president of Harvard (1869-1909), had been a tireless campaigner for reform of education, having traveled the country arguing in its favor at the turn of the century, eventually being rewarded with a position directly on the board of Rockefeller's GEB. It is not necessary to read the entirety of Mr. Eliot's paper, for the corrupted fool says nothing more in the ensuing 29 pages than he does in the first two sentences, which read: "The best part of all human knowledge has come by exact and studied observation through the senses of sight, hearing, taste, smell and touch. The most important part of education has always been the training of the senses through which that best part of human knowledge comes."[20] In other words, this Harvard-educated, one-time Harvard president was arguing for a denial of any principled education, and its replacement by that of empiricism. No longer would students be encouraged to ask "why," they needed only to observe what "is." *Our children were to be taught to think like animals.*

Hard on the heels of this declaration of national menticide, the detailed outline of the new curriculum

Abraham Flexner

was spelled out by GEB board member Abraham Flexner, in a paper titled, "A Modern School." In what the *New York Times* immediately condemned as "radical and dangerous," Flexner argued that no longer should education strive to "train the mind" of students to think in "words and abstractions" (otherwise known as ideas), which Flexner now argued were "remote from use and experience." A modern education, he said, "must produce *sheer intellectual power*, [because] our problems involve indeed concrete data and present themselves in concrete forms." Forcing the classical system to essentially justify its own existence, Flexner demanded that, "Modern education will include nothing simply because tradition recommends it or because its inutility has not been conclusively established. It proceeds in precisely the opposite way: It includes nothing for which an affirmative case cannot now be made out." (emphasis added)

Studies deemed by Flexner (and Rockefeller) to embody an excess of "inutility," and were thus to be tossed by the wayside of history, included the study of classical languages, Latin and Greek—if anyone really wants to pursue those "ancient" texts, Flexner argued, "suitable translations" were sure to be found. In addition, the Modern School would "[have] the courage not to read obsolete and uncongenial classics," nor would it "hesitate to take the risk to mental discipline involved in dropping the study of formal grammar," as well as the studies of English, history, and literature. What would take its place? "The Modern School," he wrote, "should be a *laboratory* from which would issue scientific studies of all kinds of educational problems, a laboratory, first of all, which would test and evaluate critically the fundamental propositions on which it is itself based, and the results as they are obtained." So now, children were not just to be treated as animals, but specifically as guinea pigs.[21]

---

19. Gates, Frederick T., *The Country School of Tomorrow*, General Education Board, New York City, 1913, p. 6, 10.

20. Elliott, Charles W. "Changes Needed in American Secondary Education," found in *School and Society*, Volume III, January-June, 1916, J. McKeen Cattell, ed. p 397-407 https://books.google.com/books?id=QPJAAQAAMAAJ

21. Flexner, Abraham, "A Modern School," *American Review of Reviews* 53 (1916): 465-474. http://historymatters.gmu.edu/d/4995/

In their denunciation, appearing the day immediately after news of Flexner's "School" became public, on January 21, 1917, the *Times* further condemned this program as "bread-and-butter education," adding that, "there is not a trace of anything tending to the development of character. There is nothing that would lead us to suppose that the graduate of the 'modern school' would have in his mind any ideas, and general ideas, any ideas at all above or outside the realm of his daily tasks." Further calling the program "unblushing materialism," they said, it contained "not a spiritual thought, not an idea that rises above the need of finding money for the pocket and food for the belly." Adding to the urgency behind the denunciation by the *Times*, was that Rockefeller was now willing to put the astounding sum of $35,000,000—the approximate sum of his combined national reform givings, thus far—behind this *single school*, with Flexner's additional—almost threatening—statement that they (the Rockefeller-financed philanthropoids) would do "whatever it takes," to make this program a reality.[22]

With Flexner behind this effort—thereby armed with Rockefeller's money—the *Times'* worries were well founded. Flexner had just overseen a complete overhaul of the "health care" system of the entire nation (this done with the assistance of Carnegie money), implementing the same reductionist instruction methods for the nation's medical schools which the philanthropoids had done in general education (details of which he had published in a 1910 study, the *Flexner Report*), and having earlier authored his own critique of education, *The American College*, in 1908. Although Flexner had worried about the "chicken and the egg" problem, i.e., where would the teachers for this new program come from, it was a straw man argument; the teachers already existed, in the form of the new psychology programs Rockefeller's money had

Library of Congress

John Dewey

already promoted, at the breeding grounds of the University of Chicago and New York's Columbia University. The oligarchical philanthropoids were ready to build a playground where grown men could play with the minds of young children. They called them psychologists and they called it the Lincoln Experimental School.

120th and Broadway

If there is one word to describe the life and ideas of John Dewey, it would be "pragmatism." While he did not invent the discipline, with his prolific verbal and written output he certainly became its leading American proponent, arguing that the value of an idea was judged by its "usefulness," another word for utilitarianism. Coming out of Johns Hopkins University in 1884 as a student of Hegel and Kant, Dewey was also exposed early to the ideas of British naturalist Thomas Huxley, the man who would come to be known as "Darwin's bulldog," applying this empirical, imperial view to human evolution. Any early idealism Dewey may have had[23] was to be quickly abandoned when, after teaching for two years at the University of Michigan, Dewey was led to Rockefeller's University of Chicago, where the environment was ready for him to put into practice his developing theories of education. In 1896, in addition to forming the Chicago Philosophy Club (a salon for University instructors), Dewey, along with his wife, Alice Chapman Dewey, formed the Laboratory School where they would, over the next eight years, lead several hundreds of students/teachers to experiment daily with a small group of elementary school students which they treated like guinea pigs, cataloging their every move.

Dewey turned the notion of teaching, where formerly the teacher imparted knowledge which the student absorbed and then replicated, on its head, and in-

---

22. "Radical and Dangerous," *New York Times*, Jan. 21, 1917, ProQuest Historical Newspapers (1851-2011), p. E2.

23. In 1888, Dewey wrote a 200-page critique of Leibniz's *New Essays Concerning the Human Understanding*, wherein he defended Leibniz over Locke, but in the context of German philosophy over British, arguing that Kant was an heir of the Leibniz tradition!

stead saw the process as one where the teacher was to use the innate curiosity of a child to *draw from the child* whatever the child might contain within him, and nothing more. "The primary root of all educative activity," Dewey wrote in 1890, "is in the instinctive, impulsive attitudes and activities of the child."[24] In 1898, in his first work of national acclaim, *The School and Society*, Dewey argued that the schools needed to *recreate the experience of life on the farm* (which was then being lost because of rapid urbanization) because it was in the performance of manual farm labor that the child learned the most.

> No number of object-lessons, got up as object-lessons for the sake of giving information, can afford even the shadow of a substitute for acquaintance with the plants and animals of the farm and garden, acquired through actual living among them and caring for them. No training of sense-organs in school, introduced for the sake of training, can begin to compete with the alertness and fullness of sense-life that comes through daily intimacy and interest in familiar occupations.[25]

Beyond that, Dewey additionally worked to undermine the independent thinking of the individual child, arguing that, "The primary business of school is to *train children in cooperative and mutually helpful living, to foster in them the consciousness of interdependence*, and to help them practically in making the adjustments that will carry this spirit into overt deeds." (emphasis added)

In 1905, after a clash (possibly contrived) with University of Chicago president Rainey Harper over control of his Laboratory School, Dewey resigned his position and almost immediately accepted an offer to join the Philosophy Department at the "University of the House of Morgan," a.k.a. Columbia University in New York, now under control of newly installed president, Nicholas Murray Butler. There, Dewey then was at the center of the progressive psychology movement of the nation, a resource which Rockefeller's $35,000,000 would soon put to use, in another laboratory setting.

The Lincoln School formally opened its doors in 1917, with John Dewey's pragmatic ideas at its center. Originally located in the up-scale west side of Manhattan, it quickly moved to its permanent location at 120th and Broadway, as an annex of Teachers College, on the sprawling Columbia University campus (land originally donated by Cornelius Vanderbilt, according to its website). Keeping with Dewey's philosophy of not "forcing" knowledge into the child, the school did not formally teach even the alphabet, reading or writing, basic math, or history. The school did not hand out "grades" in the sense in which we know them, for he argued that that would tend to foster "competitive individualism," something which the whole experiment was intended to destroy.

In the words of an exuberant director[26] of Teachers College, "The Lincoln School's impact on the nation was monumental. The faculty published volumes; they developed curricula and field-tested them in cooperating public schools. They helped to overhaul school systems in Pittsburgh, Denver, Cleveland, Baltimore, Rochester, Chicago, and St. Louis." In 1923, Teachers College created an International Institute which brought additional thousands of recruits to its doors, extending its reach worldwide. Among its notable graduates: John D. Rockefeller, Jr. had sent his three boys—David, Lawrence and Nelson—to the school (likely as an endorsement). Ironically, all three complained, even into adulthood, that they had difficulty reading, since they had never been formally taught in school.

Dewey was present at the creation of numerous professional organizations, many of which are still active today. In 1899, he was central to the founding of the American Psychiatric Association;[27] then, in 1905, the American Philosophical Association. At the time of the formation of the Lincoln School, Dewey was part of another Manhattan-based education reform operation, this one in secondary education, called the New School for Social Research, a project on which Dewey worked directly with Bertrand Russell, himself.[28]

24. Dewey, John, in "Froebel's Educational Principles," unpublished manuscript, Elementary School Record, No. I, February, 1900. Quoted in *The Dewey School: The Laboratory School of the University of Chicago, 1896-1903*, by [teachers] Katherine Camp Mayhew and Anna Camp Edwards (New York: D. Appleton-Century Co., London,1936).
25. Dewey, John, *The School and Society* (Chicago, Illinois: University of Chicago Press, 1900, page 24. https://ia801408.us.archive.org/33/items/schoolsociety00dewerich/schoolsociety00dewerich.pdf

26. An uncredited speech of the self-identified "tenth president" [thought to be its current president, Susan Fuhrman] of Teachers College, posted on its website: http://www.tc.columbia.edu/news/6044
27. Yes, this is the same group which signed off on Dick Cheney's CIA torture program in 2003.
28. http://www.newschool.edu/nssr/history/

Shortly after the Lincoln Experimental School opened, in 1919, Dewey went on a trip to Japan, and eventually China, giving an estimated 200 lectures during a stay that lasted two years. In 1926, we find him helping to reform the schools in Mexico, and in 1934 in South Africa. Dewey also circulated his ideas by producing dozens of articles in cooperative media outlets such as the *Nation* and the *New Republic*. He would officially remain at the school until he retired in 1930; his experiment lasted another ten years before it too, was shuttered. But by then, the damage had been done.

Rewriting History, Destroying Scientific Research

By the mid-1920s, the effects of Rockefeller's and Carnegie's money had come to influence the education of an entire generation of our nation's youth, many of whom were then approaching adulthood. Dewey's school produced the next layer of educational leaders. From here our story could go in many directions. The number of foundations began to grow at an exponential rate, with their "tainted" money having an increasingly corrupting influence on a wider and wider scope. In 1923, Rockefeller money (primarily through the $74,000,000 Laura Spellman Rockefeller Memorial Fund that J.D. Rockefeller, Sr. created to commemorate the passing of his wife in 1918) was behind the formation of the Social Science Research Council (SSRC), providing a national showcase for Dewey's "psychotic" networks. The SSRC was championed as the first "interdisciplinary science" institution in the modern age. It most importantly brought together the imperial "science" of anthropology, along with history and psychology (a representative of each being permanently on the board) and also included mathematics, sociology, and political science. In the words of one researcher, "Not bound by the specific combinations of faculty at any one university or research center, the Council drew researchers from around the country and increasingly around the world to create interdisciplinary teams defined by specific themes and able to push intellectual frontiers."

Norman Dodd, lead congressional investigator of the takeover of education by the foundations.

Here one has to stop a moment and reflect: By the power and actions of Wall Street, the concept of "knowledge" had been first broken up into specialized "disciplines," with the justification that a "unification" of these compartmentalized studies would somehow yield back the universal whole which had been originally severed. Yet, here, with the SSRC, we have the proof that the Aristotelian sum of the parts will never equal the indivisible whole. The entire concept of "science" was now to be dominated by "social" constructs, determined—not even by empirical "facts"—but by oligarchical whim (meaning money) and "confirmed" by *consensus*—surveys subjected to statistical analysis.

The entire concept of Universal Truth had been totally destroyed.

Another critical example would be the American History Association (AHA). For the story behind the formation and initial purpose of the AHA (still in existence today), we have the words of one Norman Dodd, the lead investigator for the 1953 Congressional "Reece" Committee (about which we will soon learn more), which strongly challenged the foundation world. In 1982, an aging but otherwise very credible Dodd spoke with radio journalist Ed Griffin, for his show *The Reality Zone*, and revealed this story: After World War One, a goal of the foundations was to ensure that the United States never returned to the *status quo ante*— where the British were our enemies—and that to ensure that, the foundations set the astonishing goal of *rewriting the known history* of the United States. Discovered during an exceptionally rare in-person review of Carnegie Endowment archives from the 1920s, by Dodd's research associate Katherine Casey, here is how Dodd described her shocking findings:

> So they [the Carnegie philanthropoids] approach four of the then-most prominent teachers of American history in the country—people like Charles and Mary Beard—and their suggestion to them is: will they alter the manner in which they present their subject? And they got turned

down flat. So they then decide that it is necessary for them to do as they say, "build our own stable of historians."

Then they approach the Guggenheim Foundation, which specializes in fellowships, and say: 'When we find young men in the process of studying for doctorates in the field of American history and we feel that they are the right caliber, will you grant them fellowships on our say-so?' And the answer is yes. So, under that condition, eventually they assembled twenty, and they take this twenty potential teachers of American history to London, and there they're briefed on what is expected of them when, as, and if they secure appointments in keeping with the doctorates they will have earned. That group of twenty historians ultimately becomes the nucleus of the American Historical Association.

Toward the end of the 1920's, the Endowment grants to the American Historical Association $400,000 for a study of our history in a manner which points to what can this country look forward to in the future. That culminates in a seven-volume study, the last volume of which is, of course, in essence a summary of the contents of the other six. The essence of the last volume is: The future of this country belongs to collectivism administered with characteristic American efficiency. That's the story that ultimately grew out of and, of course, was what could have been presented by the members of this Congressional committee to the Congress as a whole for just exactly what it said. They [the Committee] never got to that point.[29]

Now, in any other context, the attempt to alter the perception of the individual of his or her personal or collective past, with the aim of achieving certain behavioral modifications in the future would be called *brain-washing*. When its done by a group with an official-sounding title, however, with lots of establishment "bling" about it, it is somehow accepted as authoritative. Had the institutions of the nation been weakened to such a point?

An additional aspect of control, previously touched on, is that, from their very inception, foundations learned to function this way—by committee, thereby both increasing the anonymity, and decreasing the accountability of the individual—on every level which they operated. Grants, as well as the boards which disseminated them, were not made to (or by) individual people, but to (and by) a *group*, the better to increase conformity (and restrict independent thinking) on both ends. Johns Hopkins researcher Curt Richter well described this phenomenon, as it would play out in the days after World War II. Richter said:

> In making application for a grant before World War II, a few lines or at most a paragraph or two sufficed for the experimental design; now it may extend over six to eight single-spaced typewritten pages. And even then committee members may come back for more details. Under these circumstances, passing the buck has come to be practiced very widely. Projects are passed from Committee to Committee—to my knowledge, in one instance six Committees—largely because at no place along the line did any one believe that he had adequate information to come to a firm decision.[30]

Reflecting on the chilling implications of this for scientific research, Rene Wormser, head of research for the 1950's Reece Committee, wrote the following in 1958:

> The control imposed on a scientist by the requirement that his research designs be approved by the members of numerous giant committees will bring his ideas down to the lowest intellectual common denominator. It will impose on him the most powerful pressure to conform to a pattern of mediocrity. Whyte [William Whyte, in

---

29. Dodd continued to relate how the discovery of the existence of such extensive subversion, by an otherwise unassuming American, quite literally drove Miss Casey crazy: "I might tell you, this experience, as far as its impact on Katherine Casey was concerned, was she never was able to return to her law practice… Ultimately, she lost her mind as a result of it. It was a terrible shock. It's a very rough experience to encounter proof of these kinds." Fortunately for history, Mr. Griffin's entire one-hour interview with Mr. Dodd is preserved on YouTube, and can be viewed at https://www.youtube.com/watch?v=YUYCBfmIcHM

30. Whyte, William, *The Organization Man* (Simon & Schuster, 1956). Quoted in Wormser, Rene, *Philanthropic Foundations, Their Power and Influence*, 1958 pp. 25-26.

his 1956 book, *Organization Man*] ridicules the argument presented for scientific teamwork: that the group, even in the realm of thought, is superior to the individual. The foundations have not responded to the challenge to invigorate individual research.

It is no wonder that so many creative individuals have been conditioned to abandon individual projects. The climate produced in the world of ideas by the large foundations, upon whose support so many scholars must rely for research, is not favorable to individual projects. Such scholars are often seduced into group research because of the difficulty of getting individual grants and because of the financial lure of generous foundation subsidy for large projects. This lure draws many away from potentially creative work and the pursuit of new discovery, and leads them into sterile fields tended by conformists.[31]

Whyte's book, Wormser said, revealed that this "grope think" reduced the very topics which would be considered for scientific research, and "threaten(ed) in the end to destroy all vestiges of genius, individual responsibility and initiative, and with them the concepts of individual independence and liberty so dear to earlier generations."

And this is how it continued, more or less uninterrupted, under the guidance of philanthropic money and program, throughout the Depression and until well after World War II. At that point, the philanthropic world of the Wall Street privatized *fondi* were about to take a giant leap, both in size and scope of activity, with the "overnight" infusion of some unearned millions, that in the name of the Ford Foundation.

Blood and Circuses

In 1943, Edsel Ford, only son of the Ford founder Henry Ford, died of stomach cancer, at the age of 49. The event so traumatized his father that, four years later, Henry Ford, after briefly managing to retake control of the company Wall Street had taken away from him, would also succumb to death. Between the two of them, the formerly backwoods Ford Foundation (char-

Rowan Gaither

tered in the state of Michigan in 1936) was soon to find itself in possession of 90% of the non-voting stock of the Ford Motor Company, with an estimated street value just short of $500,000,000. With the funds expected to clear probate in 1949, just as President Truman's United States was flexing its wings as the new imperial ruler of the post-World War II free world, a pile of unaccountable money of this size would come in handy. Things started to happen.

In 1949, the Rand Corporation was formed in Pasadena, California, as a privatized spin-off of United States wartime intelligence operations. The man they put in charge of the operation was attorney Rowan Gaither, himself an OSS man who had spent World War II in charge of the critical Radiation Lab, a highly classified joint British-American radar research project at MIT. In 1946, Gaither is said to have approached Henry Ford and impressed him to the point of being hired by the foundation, where Gaither quickly took control, becoming president in 1953. For 10 critical years, then (until he retired in 1961), Rowan Gaither had charge of two of the most influential non-governmental Cold War institutions: Rand and the Ford Foundation. Between 1948 and 1950, Ford "loaned" a total of $1,000,000 to Rand; in 1952, it forgave the loans, turning them into grants. From this beginning, Ford went on to spearhead the financing of many imperial Cold War operations of the new guardians of the free world, something it did in close cooperation with the

---

31. Wormser, ibid, p. 230. https://archive.org/stream/ShadowGovernmentAndBankingEliteTopSecret145/Foundations-Their-Power-and-Influence-by-Rene-A-Wormser-438_djvu.txt

newly-formed Central Intelligence Agency and increasing coordination with London's MI6.[32]

Even given that awesome global responsibility, Ford did not neglect domestic programs. As one of his first orders of business, Gaither established a blue-ribbon committee, composed of himself (a lawyer and former president of Pacific National Bank), six former or current university presidents (including both a "natural" and a "political" scientist), and a foundation director, which spent one full year looking for ways to use their large amounts of cash infusions in such a way that they could best be used to expand their work of social manipulation. The resulting Gaither Report concluded that five vaguely defined areas—World Peace, Freedom and Democracy, Economic Development, Education, and Scientific Advancement—should be targeted.

While Ford money was supporting clandestine CIA-approved projects around the world, it was Rockefeller's money which was about to create another big devolution domestically—giving Americans a diversion from the tensions of the escalating Cold War—with the publication, in 1948, of Alfred Kinsey's report on the *Sexual Behavior in the American Male*.

Alfred Kinsey had been on the Rockefeller payroll since 1941, working at the National Research Council (NRC), originally funded through the Bureau of Social Hygiene (BSH)—a personal project of John D. Rockefeller, Jr., dating from 1911—and, after 1921, by the Rockefeller Foundation directly. The first BSH study, which defined its work for the next decades, was a profile of the prostitution "industry" in New York City. Kinsey's elevation as a researcher represented the triumph of the "sociologists" over the "scientific" investi-

Alfred Kinsey

gations at the NRC, under their Committee for Research in Problems of Sex. Using a voluntary survey technique, highly criticized for its unrepresentative make-up, Kinsey succeeded in doing what the medical doctors (scientists, who had a higher standard of "proof" than the statistical correlation of the sociologists) had been unable to accomplish: starting a sexual revolution. Between this—his report on the *Sexual Habits of the American Female* came out in 1953—and the Ford Foundation funded social programs, another backlash was about to erupt.

A Tale of Two Committees

Between 1952 and 1954, Congress, in what was almost certainly a historic first, mounted two separate investigations, each accompanied with its own set of public hearings, into philanthropic foundations. The two could not have been more different. In what should be a cautionary tale to today's policy makers—consumed, one might even say blinded as they are by the "Russiagate" polemics—the first investigation (known as the "Cox Committee," named after Representative E. Eugene Cox (D-Ga.) became directed more by the burgeoning "anti-Russia" Cold War politics of the day, than an honest pursuit of the truth. Directed by a House resolution to "determine which such foundations and organizations are using their resources for un-American and subversive activities,"[33] the hearings of the Select Committee to Investigate Tax-Exempt Foundations additionally suffered in that its approach was to take testimony from the foxes who guarded the henhouse, in the form of the chairmen and directors of the foundations themselves. Then, in the second death of a Congressional leader in a month, the 72-year-old Cox died of a heart attack.

---

32. Sources on Gaither and the history of the Ford Foundation are understandably hard to find. Sources once located are today not available. One article managing to survive the bleaching of time on the Internet is "Ford Foundation, a philanthropic facade for the CIA, by Paul Labarique, viewable at https://www.voltairenet.org/article30039.html

33. *Select Committee to Investigate Tax-Exempt Foundations and Comparable Organizations*, House of Representatives, Eighty-Second Congress Second Session (US Government Printing Office: Washington, D.C., 1954), p. 1.

The issue, however, would not go away.

In 1953, following an election which threw the control of the Congress to the Republicans, the House voted 211-113 (including 69 Democrats) to mount a *second* investigation, this one under the direction of Rep. B. Carroll Reece (R-Tenn.) who had been on the failed Cox Committee, but this time with the additional mandate to examine whether foundations had acted, *"for political purposes; propaganda,* or attempts to influence legislation."* (emphasis added) In circumstances not dissimilar to today, these hearings took place with the chaotic noise of Cold War red-baiting of Senator Joe McCarthy, literally in the shadows of the HUAC hearings. The Special Committee took over 20 days of raucous public testimony in May and June of 1954, this time giving full voice to foundation critics.

While impossible to fully encapsulate them within these pages, issues central to the investigation were interlocking directorates between the Rockefeller Foundation and General Education Board, Carnegie's Foundation for the Advancement of Teaching, and his Endowment for International Peace, Ford Foundation and its Fund for the Republic, and the Rand Foundation; curriculum subversion of/by the National Education Association; activities of the Rockefeller-funded Social Science Research Council; and the League for Industrial Democracy.

Lead Investigator Norman Dodd gave this summary in his opening report:

> [O]ur study of these entities and their relationship to each other seems to warrant the inference that *they constitute a highly efficient, functioning whole.* Its product is apparently an educational curriculum designed to indoctrinate the American student from matriculation to the consummation of his education. It contrasts sharply with the freedom of the individual as the cornerstone of our social structure. For this freedom, it seems to substitute the group, the will of the majority,

Congressman Wright Patman held hearings on tax exempt foundations from 1962, and won a tax on the foundations.

and a centralized power to enforce this will—presumably in the interest of all. Its development and production seems to have been largely the work of those organizations engaged in research, such as the Social Science Research Council and the National Research Council...

In these fields the specialists, more often than not, seem to have been concerned with the production of empirical data and with its application. *Principles and their truth or falsity seem to have concerned them very little.*

In what appears from our studies to have been zeal for a radically new social order in the United States, many of these social science specialists apparently gave little thought to either the opinions or the warnings of those who were convinced that *a wholesale acceptance of knowledge acquired almost entirely by empirical methods would result in a deterioration of moral standards* and a disrespect for principles. Even past experience which indicated that such an approach to the problems of society could lead to tyranny, appears to have been disregarded.[34] (emphasis added)

Rene Wormser, the General Council for the Committee, in 1958, after seeing the hearings first cut short and then completely buried by the media (and Congress, which made not a single legislative move against the foundations) wrote a book, *Philanthropic Foundations: Their Power and Influence,* in an attempt to get the story out. The aged Norman Dodd, Research Director for the Committee, finally determined to get his untold version out, as we have seen. Wayne Hays, a Democratic Congressman from Ohio, confessed on his deathbed that he had been deployed by Sam Rayburn to

---

34. Dodd, Norman, *The Dodd Report to the Reece Committee on Foundations* (The Long House, Inc.: New York, N.Y., 1954), p. 4, and in Special Committee to Investigate Tax-Exempt Foundations, Part 1, p. 47.

McGeorge Bundy

disrupt the hearings in any way possible. Eugene Cox had perished in his original effort, and Kathryn Casey had gone insane. Such were the visible casualties of this undeclared war. Less visible was the destruction done to the minds of our fellow citizens.

With foundation power again able to suppress any legislative penalties, even after such high Congressional drama, the forces of finance could easily think that they had vanquished their degenerated foe. Then they overreached.

Their Victory: Our Defeat

Following the Presidential election of 1968, *Time* magazine suddenly revealed that eight former staffers of the recently assassinated Robert F. Kennedy campaign had been on the payroll of the Ford Foundation, having received a total of $131,000 in grants during the campaign. This major blunder by the foundations also happened to coincide with the ongoing crusade of Texas Congressman Wright Patman (D), who had been carrying on a lone battle against "Yankee" foundations on the basis of tax avoidance, since 1962. Patman, who immediately called for public hearings, had previously convinced the Treasury Department to produce a report, which they did in 1965, and, although it largely defended tax exempt foundations as "useful," upheld many of his charges of abuse. The fact that McGeorge Bundy who, in 1966, had jumped ship from the Johnson administration only to land comfortably in the chairmanship of the Ford Foundation, had testified before Patman's committee, expressing erudite disdain for "Congressional meddling" into affairs which they ought not concern themselves with, did not help matters.[35]

In the revolutionary environment of the 1960s, Congress acted, passing the Tax Act of 1969, which placed a not insignificant 4% tax on foundation holdings; a restriction on direct connections with private businesses; and a minimum annual payout percentage of 6% of holdings. However, the primary weapon, a limit on perpetuity, in the form of a 25-year payout requirement—strong calls for which had come from Patman as well Republican Senator Al Gore, Sr, then head of the Senate Finance Committee—was defeated on the Senate floor (and was thus removed from the bill in its final form).[36] The 4% tax ultimately enacted had been whittled down from Patman's proposed 7.5% and was further reduced to 2% in the Deficit Reduction bill, signed by President Ronald Reagan in 1984.

In panicked response to this unexpected up-swelling of republican spirit, the foundations scrambled to put their house in order. Their internal report, done by the "independent" Council on Foundations, headed by former president of Carnegie Corporation John Gardner, issued a "clear warning" to foundations of hostile attitudes then present in both houses of Congress, but also in the public at large, further cautioning the elitist money masters of the "inherent fragility" of their position in the social order, despite the billions at their command. "Few persons associated with foundations

---

35. The career of McGeorge Bundy is worth noting, in that it is not unusual for a philanthropoid: Yale degree in 1940, army intelligence during World War II, policy analyst for the Council on Foreign Relations from 1948-49, Harvard dean from 1953-61, special assistant to the President for national security from 1961-66 (during the buildup in Vietnam), president of the Ford Foundation from 1966-79 (during the creation of the "anti-war" movement), and finally with Carnegie from 1990 until his death in 1996.

36. Leading the fight in defense of the foundation's right to tax-exempt status, was Minnesota Senator (and future vice-president) Walter Mondale.

realized, until last year, the extent of the decline in public esteem" the foundations had incurred, Gardner said, being quoted in the *New York Times*, May 28, 1970.[37]

Beyond a mostly self-serving public relations push, the foundations' ultimate response was to create, in the 1970s, what were variously called "alternative" or "activist" philanthropy: Initiating the use of cut-out and pass-through "middle man" foundations to mask the actual origin of the funds. From this were born radical funding networks, beginning with the Haymarket Fund in Boston, the Tides Foundation in San Francisco and ACORN, founded by 1960's radical student activist Wayne Rathke in Arkansas. More recently, but based on the same model, we have the Democracy Alliance, a pass-through front for liberal activists' cash, a vehicle preferred by leading anglophile billionaire George Soros. Soon, "conservative" foundations were born, as the further factionalization of the nation by its enemies continued to expand.

Epilogue

Private philanthropical foundations have now been in existence for the better part of the entire history of our United States of America. According to the Foundation Center (a resource database mandated by the Patman legislation), there are now over 86,000 foundations in this country, the vast majority (92%) of which are "private," with a value over $712,000,000,000, that's three quarters of one *trillion* dollars in assets (2014 figures). Although they are a small percentage compared to the federal budget, they are the proverbial "tail that wags the dog" as far as leading social "change"—and thus the direction in which the country moves—is concerned. The former colossal Ford Foundation, with its $11 billion in assets, is now a distant number two on the list, virtually dwarfed by number one, the (former Microsoft co-founder) Bill and Melinda Gates Foundation's $42 billion.[38] From its website, we find that the effort to "Enhance education through innovation" (and no doubt through the sale of Windows computers) is still one of the top priorities.

It has now been more than four generations that the British, working through their Wall Street philanthropoid agents, have so weakened the minds of the citizens of our once revered republic to the point of self-inflicted mental slavery, and almost two generations since our elected representatives took any meaningful action against them. In that short span of 100 years' time *we have seen our country's "mission" in the world turned on its head, both domestically and worldwide.* Today, the existence of foundations is rarely noted (except in "alternative" media). Their *right* to existence is no longer even questioned. Ever since the onset of the "generation gap," in the 1960s, society has been robbed of any historical notion of its existence, with all ties to previous generations written off as, "that was then," and "that's sooo 20th Century," as if the laws of the Universe now change with each passing generation. Through the work of foundation-funded sociological researchers, society has been robbed of that historical continuity, lumping us instead into sociological constructs such as Baby Boomers, Gen Xers and Millennials, as opposed to citizens of a great republic, with roots tracing back over 500 years. Sociologists have additionally taught us how to speak—another constriction on the thought process—through notions such as Political Correctness, Multiculturalism, and now Identity Politics.

And, while everyone realizes that our education system is failing us, as long as educators (and politicians) approach their human subjects as some sort of cross between a monkey and a computer (the way they themselves have been taught), we will go from one (Bush-era No Child Left Behind) program to another (Obama-era The Race to the Top), each time getting poorer results, and not knowing why. The first step in fixing education is to acknowledge what a child *is*, and why we would educate one in the first place. Not to fill the time during which two parents struggle to make a living, but rather because a child is *human*, and it is both possible and necessary for our species' survival that successive generations of humanity *transcend themselves* by future generations learning from the past—both successes and failures.

When teachers recognize that "genius" is a natural state of human existence, and not something to be dulled by ritalin, we will have begun to take our nation back.

---

37. Council on Foundations, History. See entry for 1970. https://www.cof.org/sites/default/files/documents/files/History-Council-on-Foundations.pdf

38. In 2006, Warren Buffet, the second-richest man in the world, donated his entire riches to Bill Gates, creating this "super" foundation.

June 22, 2006

'I Don't Believe in Signs'

by Lyndon H. LaRouche, Jr.

The world as a whole is currently impelled toward threatened, early, general, physical breakdown-crisis of the trans-Atlantic monetary-financial system. The breakdown itself could be averted by methods which amount to a return to the outlook expressed in the great reforms made by President Franklin Delano Roosevelt. If that needed reform is to be brought about, the special impediment which must be overcome, is found in the fact that the generation now dominating current trans-Atlantic power centers, that born between, approximately, the close of World War II and the onset of the steep recession of 1957-1958, has lost two earlier generations' essential connections to those lessons of the Franklin Roosevelt recovery and the 1939-1945 war which had been crucial for the defeat of Hitler's empire, connections which were also indispensable for the recovery which followed during the immediate two post-war decades.

The kernel of the disorientation which pervades among the pace-setters of today's currently reigning, upper twenty percentile of political and economic power, is the delusion known by such currently popular titles as "information theory," "post-industrial society," "post-modernism," and "globalization." It is presently urgent that those currently reigning expressions of Sophistry be identified as such, and that the contrary, appropriate measures for returning society to relative mental health be adopted.

On that subject, about six years back, the late, redoubtable Mark Burdman referred my attention to a book, Doron Swade's **The Cogwheel Brain**, which, at Mark's prompting, I reviewed for **EIR** at that time.[1] As Swade's title frankly implies, that book, although authored by a writer with specialist credentials, was also notable for its expressed character as a piece influenced by post-modernist modes in Sophistry, as this was expressed in its representation of the Charles Babbage whose conceptions are the root of the Twentieth-Century development of the electronic computer.[2] The issues which Mark posed for my attention then, have a new kind of relevance for the rising new adult generation of today,

Mark's following message to me is still notable today on that account. I repeat it now:

"I think you will find this book both interesting and infuriating. You can do with it as you wish.

"I have read it through and found the 'story line' compelling, but the author is either uninformed, or crazy on basic scientific/epistemological matters, e.g., with his page 84 equating Leibniz and von Neumann, as both mathematicians involved with 'symbols,' and so on.

"Swade, the author, repeatedly mentions Babbage's ties to the European continent, with [Alexander] von Humboldt, French circles that are descended from Lazare Carnot, etc.; but, this is never developed in any detail. Swade is obviously uncomfortable, and perhaps angry, with Babbage's attacks on English science, in his 1830 writing, **Reflections on the Decline of Science in England**, and elsewhere.

"Swade is a key guy in something in Britain called the 'Information Age Project,' founded in the 1970s,

---

1. Lyndon LaRouche, "Who Was Charles Babbage?" **EIR**, May 19, 2000.

2. Doron Swade, **The Cogwheel Brain** (London: Little, Brown and Company, 2000). Cf. Philip and Emily Morrison, **Charles Babbage and His Calculating Engines: Selected Writings by Charles Babbage and Others** (Dover Publications, 1961).

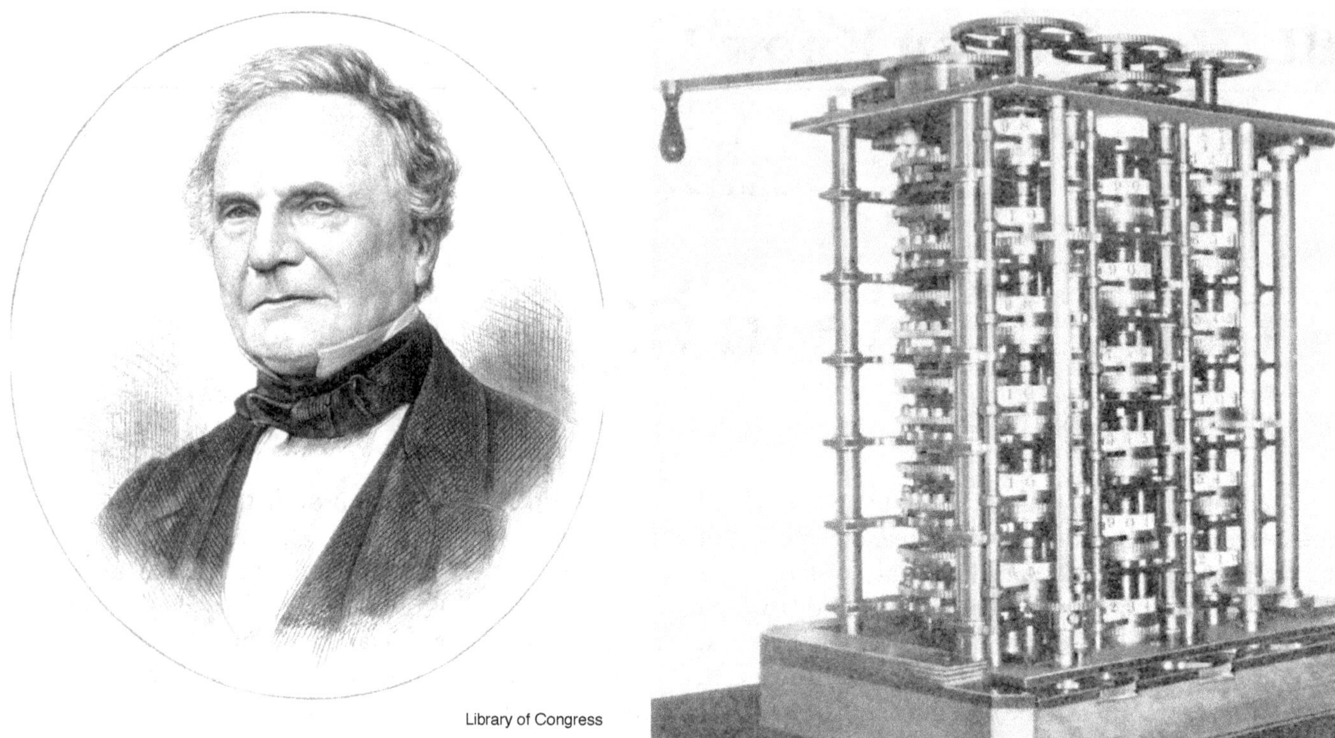

Charles Babbage (1791-1871) and his Difference Engine. The importance of emphasizing "the Charles Babbage lurking within the design of every competently functional, modern digital computing system," LaRouche writes, "is that there is no magical distinction in principle of underlying conception, between the original, root conception for future computing machinery by Babbage, and the most modern such electronic device."

about which we have to find out more. He gets very involved in what seems to me, in any case, to be a phony discussion, about whether the modern computer owes a great deal to Babbage, or not. I say 'phony,' because even from the evidence of this book, Babbage made fundamental contributions in other vital areas, such as machine tools, manufactures, engineering, etc. Obviously, he is someone of considerable importance, still at this moment, with the present British discussion, post-Third Way, about the destruction of real industry.

"I was also pleased, that the book never mentions Darwin, T. Huxley, etc., since almost any book these days on 'English Science' starts from these creatures.

"Anyway, I hope you find it interesting.—Mark."

I did: then, and, as you shall see, now.

Since then, a new generation of young adults has emerged as a significant force in political life, thus, hopefully, establishing new foundations for the leadership of our society over the coming half-century, or longer. So, the core of the argument which I made in that review, should be restated now, but with the inclusion of new terms of reference, terms cohering with that

refreshed approach to science occupying the emerging adult generation typified by the LaRouche Youth Movement (LYM).

The point to be made here is, given today's existential degree of world-wide policy crisis, that we proceed, as relentlessly as may be necessary to do that job, to defend the future fate of humanity against one of today's most popularized, and most ruinous hoaxes, the delusion examined in these pages under the title of so-called "information theory."

In referring to that hoax called "information theory," I am emphasizing the destructive effect, on the mind, and on the world economy, of the widespread influence of the body of pseudo-scientific dogma spread, under sundry labels, as the influence of persons such as Bertrand Russell, Norbert Wiener, and John von Neumann. I emphasize those gentlemen's adherence to a cult which was propagated in such forms of expression as von Neumann's superstitious notions of "artificial intelligence," as that same cult is associated with such locations as the related, published work of Marvin Minsky and Noam Chomsky under the auspices of

MIT's Research Laboratory of Electronics (RLE). It was this wretched ideology, launched in the U.S.A. of the 1940s as the "Cybernetics" project of agencies such as the Josiah Macy, Jr. Foundation, which has been the crucial ideological feature of the method by which the once mighty U.S. economy, among others, has systematically destroyed itself over the course of the 1968-2006 period to date.

That use of the term "intelligence," as the term is misused by those post-modernist ideologues, expressed an intended deception. That deception expressed the intent of the circles of Bertrand Russell, Russell's acolytes Norbert Wiener and John von Neumann, and also the wretched Margaret Mead et al., to destroy the world of U.S. President Franklin Roosevelt. That was, and remains a deception which must be uprooted, lest the still spreading weeds of such delusions cripple the minds of an already all too credulous humanity, lodging them, thus, within a self-inflicted, presently threatened lurch into a new dark age: a dark age comparable to that which wiped out an estimated one-third of the population of mid-Fourteenth-Century Europe.

The most efficient treatment of that subject which I have placed at issue here, lies within a topical area, the science of physical economy, in which my special expertise in long-range economic forecasting is outstanding, on record of performance, in the world of today. It was my 1948 recognition of the central fallacy of the argument which Professor Norbert Wiener presented, in his **Cybernetics**, which led me directly to those researches of 1948-1953 which, in turn, led me to my own original discoveries which were added to the domain of Leibniz's science of physical economy. What first impelled me toward my own original, 1948-1953, discoveries in economics treated as a branch of physical science, was this 1948 recognition of the fundamental error employed by Bertrand Russell's dupe Norbert Wiener as the basis for Wiener's own, and Russell dupe John von Neumann's brutish misconception of the essential nature of the human individual.

To clear up the widespread ignorance and confusion on this subject, we must begin here by reaffirming certain essential elements of sanity respecting the origins of that modern electronic digital computer which, while, on the one side, an integral part of life today, has also been cruelly misrepresented as a potential, or even actual medium of "artificial intelligence," and has been made, thus, into a temple of worship for the devotees of a modern Sophist cult, the radically reductionist, logically-positivist sophistry of so-called "information theory."

I have made the essential argument in numerous locations over recent years, and in earlier times. This time, I restate the crucial point from a fresh standpoint, with some points added which, among other purposes served here, are crucially significant for their bearing on work, on physical-economic animations, which is ongoing at this time.

1. The Birth of the Modern Computer

The history bearing upon Babbage's most notable discoveries within what became the development of digital computer systems, is fairly summarized as follows.

The roots of those relevant strains of modern physical science in which the valid currents of modern European science were developed, are found chiefly in the implications of the founding of that modern European experimental physical science by the Fifteenth-Century *De Docta Ignorantia* of Cardinal Nicholas of Cusa.[3] This development was also expressed at that time by the crucial discoveries of such contemporaries of Cusa as the Filippo Brunelleschi who applied the catenary function to construction of the cupola of the Cathedral of Florence, and by explicit followers of Cusa, such as Leonardo da Vinci and Johannes Kepler. Cusa student Leonardo da Vinci's invention of the principle of modern weaving machines, is a particular contribution by Leonardo, which, in this instance, led into the development of the programming of computers, that by the route of Babbage's adoption of the punched-card system, for weaving, of Joseph-Marie Jacquard.

That development of scientific calculating machines, which led into the Twentieth-Century development of the general purpose electronic computer, began with the development, first, of such a machine built by Johannes Kepler, one crafted by him to assist his calcu-

---

3. The term "experimental physical science" signifies the exclusion of *apriori* assumptions, such as those associated with Euclidean, or modern reductionist mathematics and physics doctrines generally. Although anti-Euclidean physical geometries were characteristic of the work of the Pythagoreans and Plato, for example, and were prescribed by Carl F. Gauss's teacher Abraham Kästner, the explicitly thorough application of anti-Euclidean physical geometries was formally introduced by Bernhard Riemann's 1854 habilitation dissertation.

lations for astronomy. Secondly, a copy of what Kepler described as his machine, was crafted by Blaise Pascal. Thirdly, Pascal's work was the starting-point of reference for the then revolutionary technological development of the early general-purpose scientific calculator, by Gottfried Leibniz. Fourth, the development of the design for the mechanical forerunner of the modern digital computer, was chiefly a reflection of the influence of Gottfried Leibniz on Babbage's invention of the mechanical model for the modern electronic computer. Full circle, back to Kepler's astronomy: on his own account, Babbage's discovery was prompted by his continuing close personal association with Britain's leading astronomer of that time, Sir John Herschel, and also with the followers of Kepler and Leibniz among those broader European circles of Babbage's personal acquaintance, as typified by the scientist Alexander von Humboldt, the latter both in Germany and the Monge-Carnot Ecole Polytechnique program in France.

In that historical context of the time, the context of the rising influence of Carl F. Gauss's revolutionary discoveries in astronomy, Babbage's close personal association with the celebrated son of the celebrated astronomer Frederick Wilhelm Herschel, was of crucial importance in prompting Babbage's undertaking the development of designs for his mechanical calculating devices.[4] This was a reaction to a recurring problem within the work of modern astronomy: the toil of building accurate arithmetical tables: most notably, since the work of Tycho Brahe and the genius who superseded

him, Johannes Kepler. However, excepting the importance of Babbage's recognizing the utility of Jacquard's punched-card system, as a needed approach to variable programming of Babbage's design for calculating machinery, the kernel of the discovery which served as the model for his development of the approach used in modern calculating machinery, was, otherwise, contrary to the sophistries of Swade, essentially Babbage's own.

The importance for science of undertaking such mammoth calculating activity, had been made clear by the way in which Kepler recognized, and treated the errors in the work of his predecessor Tycho Brahe. Where Aristarchus of Samos had proven the Solar principle of astronomy by the method of *Sphaerics* employed by Thales et al., the study of eclipses of the Sun and Moon, Kepler not only revived the standpoint of Aristarchus, but used the Sun-Earth-Mars alignments to define an apparent margin of error in orbital characteristics of the Solar System. This apparent error required a reworking of the statistics collected by Brahe, that with the degree of precision which not only settled the issues posed by the apparently anomalous form of the Mars orbit, but demonstrated an elliptical orbit for the Earth itself. The method of Kepler was given a second, stunning proof in Carl F. Gauss's experimental proof of the Keplerian character of the asteroid "belt," a proof which reverberated among the circles of Herschel and Babbage.

Such were the challenges which the work of Carl Gauss had presented to the work of Babbage's friend and collaborator Herschel. Massive work in detecting and checking data, was now made obligatory by the successive work of Kepler and Kepler's followers through Gauss's stunning discovery of the asteroid orbits. The problems addressed were physical-geometric, not arithmetic, nor simply algebraic, in essential quality; the curvatures must be measured in detail, and this required massive calculations based on repeated observations, observations which must be measured in the precision of great detail. Additionally, it was the evidence of typical errors in the work of those employed to carry out these calculations, which impelled Babbage to discover machines which could reduce greatly this significant factor of error by human calculators in compiling of astronomical tables at that time.

The reasonable forms of debates respecting the respective validities of the design of both Babbage's intention and his machine, have usually reflected practi-

---

4. The genesis of this invention by Babbage dates from the formation of the Cambridge Analytical Society, approximately 1811, prompted by the circulation of an hilarious, but shrewd denunciation of the so-called Newton calculus, a denunciation presented in a celebrated composition written by Babbage, John Herschel, et al., under the title of "The Principles of pure D-ism in opposition to to the Dot-age of the University." The authors referenced John Herschel's celebrated father, as the German from Hannover who was the only competent mathematician in England at that time. This fact respecting the dilapidated state of science and industry in early Nineteenth-century England correlates with the fact that the young English-speaking U.S.A., which had been founded under the leadership of the scientist Benjamin Franklin, had a level of productivity approximately twice that under the British monarchy at that time. The economic power commanded by the British monarchy reposed in the strategic advantage, since February 1763, of the British East India Company's international role, in sucking the blood of much of the world outside Britain itself. Since then, the British monarchy represented, thus, an imperial form of the Anglo-Dutch Liberal system, a system which is the forerunner of what is represented by the alliance of the pro-Nazi Lazard Frères/Banque Worms circles of France with the Bilderbergers of today. (A Bilderberger is a meatball composed of an assembly of scraps of human flesh.)

cal problems of Nineteenth-Century production methods, rather than actually principled errors in Babbage's intentions. The actual difficulties had been the practical impediments, during the Nineteenth Century, to building a set of machines based on Babbage's design in England at that time, the lack of development of the required precision in then existing machine-tool practice. This practical factor is what, chiefly, delayed the construction of a full-scale Difference Engine according to the intention embodied in Babbage's design. As subsequent developments showed, only qualitative improvements in technology of production, over time, were required, to refine the physical construction of machines based on Babbage's design, in the successive steps of successful development of the so-called Hollerith machines which preceded the development of electronic digital computers.

Author Swade indulged in the sophistry of appearing to debate the question: which among the sundry known rivals and professed followers of Babbage's intention have actually claimed or denied knowledge of the predecessor's, Babbage's, designs? That issue, as posed by Swade, is best characterized as an example of flagrant sophistry.

In such matters, let the evidence speak for itself. The only honest question is, whether or not Babbage reflects the same principle on which competent modern general-purpose calculating machinery has been premised. To answer the question of how Babbage's development of his discovery was premised, and proceeded, we know, that since Babbage was prompted by the relatively recent fame of Carl Gauss's discovery of the asteroid orbits, and the fact that this accomplishment had given crucial proof of the method of Kepler against the followers of Galileo and the Newtonians, Babbage and his friend Herschel must be understood as deliberating in that context. In this light, the apparent prompting of Swade's sophistical evasions is seen, as Mark Burdman's message to me suggests: presently continuing official British hostility, in the tradition of London's Newcomen Society hoax, to Babbage's part in the authorship of both the 1811 Cambridge piece, "D-ism and Dotage," and, as Swade himself indicates, Babbage's own 1830 **Reflections on the Decline of Science in England.**

Today, the specific, continuing importance of emphasizing the Charles Babbage lurking within the design of every competently functional, modern digital computing system, is that there is no magical distinction in principle of underlying conception, between the original, root conception for future computing machinery by Babbage, and the most modern such electronic device. It is the development, applications, and implications of the electronics, which is new; the rest, the root of the matter, is traced to the conceptions employed by Babbage.

The working point in this report on that subject, is that anything lacking in principle in Babbage's own original development, is, of principled necessity, also lacking in the underlying concept of design of any digital computer-system employed today.

This limitation of computer design, then as now, is not a fault in itself. Good computers in working condition, while they still "live" their usually fragile short lives, carry out the commands uttered, in concert, by human designers, manufacturers, and operators. The problem of such computers to be examined here, is not a failure in the original conception of the digital computer itself; the fault to be corrected is typified by the case of the foolish imagination of that man, whose admiration of a department-store dummy, prompts him to propose intimacies to the poor dummy—and, perhaps, to beat the poor she-it which failed to respond with the enthusiasm which the enamored gentleman demanded.

A Sophistry by Swade

Swade's particular incompetence, is expressed in the way he purports to weigh the claims of Babbage's authorship of the principled features of digital computing machinery. This strongly suggests that either Swade was ignorant of the relevant fundamental issues of Seventeenth- through Nineteenth-Century physical science, or (in a stretch) that he, for political reasons, *had chosen to appear to be ignorant of those issues*. Putting the class of "Rube Goldberg" inventions aside, the crucial issue posed by the digital computer, whether mechanical or electronic, is the issue which places Kepler, Leibniz, Gauss, and Riemann, among others, on one side, and the empiricists and positivists, such as Descartes, Newton, D'Alembert, de Moivre, Euler, Lagrange, Cauchy, Kelvin, Clausius, Grassmann, Helmholtz, et al., on the opposing side.

The issue of the computer, as reflected in the pathological arguments of Russell, Wiener, von Neumann, Minsky, Chomsky, et al., is the issue of what de Moivre is credited as first to name "imaginary numbers." This is the issue to which we shall return attention in a later chapter of this present report. For our immediate pur-

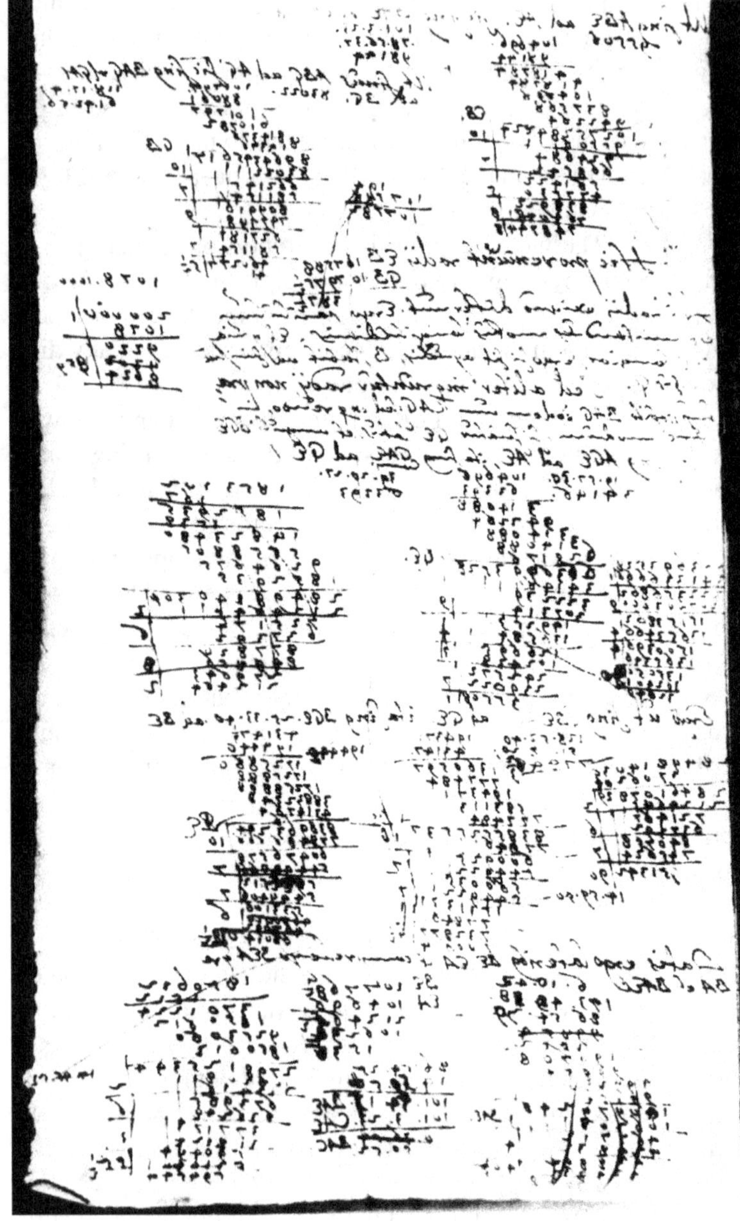

A page of Johannes Kepler's notebook shows his earliest calculations on the orbit of Mars. His notebooks are filled with laborious calculations— a strong motivation for his development of a calculating machine.

poses at this instant, it is sufficient to note that Swade's sophistry on the matter of Babbage's originality, depends implicitly upon his apparent scientific illiteracy respecting the issues of reductionist method.

There are two most notable things about the nature of Babbage's discovery itself. First, it is a true, patentable type of invention; but, we should recognize that, just as neither judges nor Monsanto are to be considered legitimately as deities, Babbage's discovery does not involve any discovery of what should be, in principle, a non-patentable discovery of a true principle found in nature, such as the discovery of genetic types. The same distinction applies to the subject of the fraudulent claims, as by both Norbert Wiener and John von Neumann, to have discovered a universal physical principle in support of their respective, fraudulent claims to discovery of the respective, non-existent principles of "information theory" as a form of "artificial intelligence."

In contrast to the duped devotees of virtual creatures cast in the likeness of creatures from the fantasy-world of H.G. Wells' Dr. Moreau, which were implicitly creatures such as those imagined by Wiener, von Neumann, et al., the crucial fact is, that individual human intelligence is the expression of an actual, distinctly specific principle of the universe, a principle corresponding to the fundamental, principled distinction, creative intelligence, of human beings from either the mere higher apes, or the ideology of those certain modern "environmentalist" politicians who monkey maliciously with mankind's destiny today. Unlike the Minsky and Chomsky who tried to make a virtual monkey of their collective self, no animal, nor machine, however elegant, might be able to exhibit an intrinsic quality of intelligence operating within the composition of that species' design.[5]

I made the relevant distinction, first, in early 1948, when I acquired loan of a pre-publication review copy of Wiener's **Cybernetics**. In part, at first, the book was delightful. Much of the gain in production techniques associated with computer technology, was identified, in germ form, within parts of Wiener's book. Yet, as much as the book had first pleased me on that account, I was soon angered by the sophistry of "Cybernetics," which Wiener had added to an otherwise interesting argument: the notion that actually human intelligence could be reduced to a Machian sophistry

5. Lest some reader lapse into an unthinking interpretation of H.G. Wells' intention in the latter's writing of that venture in "science fiction," Thomas Huxley creation Wells' moralizing intention in that novel, was to argue that do-gooders should give up trying to elevate ordinary working-class people into the status of equals to the ruling oligarchy of English-speaking society. "You will only enrage those whom you propose to elevate."

called "information theory." From that moment on, I reacted to the book, as if instinctively, with a dedication to demonstrate the deadly threat to humanity in radical reductionist Wiener's somewhat seductive "information theory" hoax.

This distinction of man from beast, defines the leading issue treated here, the issue of the inherent fraud of the claims for the alleged existence of "information" and "artificial intelligence" as principled categories of existence. However, the most certain proof of the fraud in the referenced claims of Wiener, von Neumann, et al., lies within the bounds of showing the nature of a principle of true creativity, a principle which does not exist in the systems of a reductionist mathematics such as those of the Sophist Euclid, or of such modern, empiricist successors of that Euclid as Descartes and the devotees of Sir Isaac Newton, Norbert Wiener, and John von Neumann.

Computers and Economies

Practically, the digital computer and linear programming became synonymous in the practice among many leading schools of economists and others of the early post-World War II decades. For example, as a matter of principle, the most significant among the uses of modern electronic, digital data-processing systems, from my standpoint as a physical economist, is the applications of what has been named "linear programming," as applied, for example, for governmental operations typified by Professor Wassily Leontief's contributions to the analytical correlation of the standard statistical economic reporting on national product and national income, for the purposes of assembly of the relevant U.S. government and related data.

The now recently deceased Leontief, who had been trained under the Russian Kondratieff famous for the notion of "Kondratieff Waves" in technology, did make a major contribution to the development of national accounting practice. He is distinguished from the "ivory tower" school of modern positivist radicalism by his essential sanity. However, to the best of my knowledge, he seems never to have grasped the actually dynamic nature of a truly non-linear physical-economic process. That is to say, "dynamic" in the sense of the Pythagorean *dynamis* or the definition of *dynamics* presented by Leibniz as the solution for the incompetence of the work of modern sophist René Descartes on the subject of physical science.

Strictly speaking, linear programming would always be intrinsically a failure, if it were employed as a method of medium- to long-term policy-shaping. Since it is intrinsically, ontologically, a mechanistic technique, it is axiomatically unsuited as a tool for representing a truly dynamic process of the type which any real-life economy is. Linear programming sometimes explains some bad practices of business or government management of an economic process, which is useful, but, since economic progress is intrinsically non-linear and dynamic, linear methods could never design a successful economic process.

Therefore, the inherent limitation, and potential defect attached to all forms of linear programming, is, that while the linear methods of quasi-Cartesian mechanics can report some among the effects of the application of a new principle, those methods are inherently incompetent for defining the process of change which connects what are, in physical principle, two or more successive phase-states of an economy undergoing the effects of a change in set of employed physical principles.

This is not to imply that Leontief's work itself was incompetent; quite the contrary. The question to be posed is: competent for what intended mission? Leontief himself said as much, in effect, in his late 1950s quarrel with what he described as the "ivory tower" fanatics associated with Tjalling Koopmans et al.

In principle, what Leontief charged against Koopmans et al., was not really a new issue at that time. It had already been the essential point at issue, made by Gottfried Leibniz, in pointing out the essential fraud of René Descartes' attempt at a formally mechanistic explication of what are ridiculously simple, false notions of physical principles. At issue was the error made by the defenders of Cartesian and Newtonian method, such as D'Alembert, de Moivre, Euler, Lagrange, Laplace, and Cauchy, in their fraudulent attacks on Leibniz's infinitesimal calculus and the related, subsuming principle of Leibniz's catenary-cued principle of universal physical least action. This was the issue addressed by the followers of Leibniz, such as Carl F. Gauss, against D'Alembert et al., in Gauss's 1799 doctoral dissertation.

The most characteristic feature of any actual economy, is a willful, characteristically non-linear, dynamic principle of action which is absolutely lacking in all known living species excepting the strictly definable creative powers of the individual human mind. This principle of action is expressed as the changes in econ-

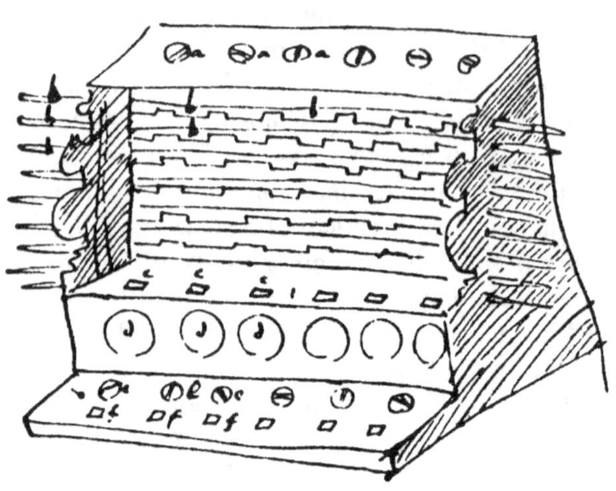

\ *Kepler's friend Wilhelm Schickart (1592-1635) was a mathematician, draughtsman, and mechanic, who built this calculating machine, following Kepler's conceptual design, in 1623. The machine was destroyed by fire, and all that remains are two sketches by Schickart. This is believed to be the first real calculating machine in the world.*

Blaise Pascal's (1623-1662) calculator was based on the principle of the Kepler-Schickart machine. It in turn was the starting-point of reference for Leibniz's calculator.

Gottfried Leibniz's (1646-1716) general-purpose scientific calculator. Babbage's invention was chiefly a reflection of the influence of Leibniz.

omy effected through the discovery and employment of a universal physical, or related principle. In all competent physical science, this same distinction is expressed as the original discovery of what appropriate tests demonstrate to be a universal physical principle.

That distinction is of crucial importance for understanding the root of the essential incompetence of any effort to treat usually taught and practiced varieties of accounting or actual economics as scientific. The crucial issue of the entire controversy is the following.

Whereas all lower forms of life, the animals most notably here, have a limit on the size of living populations, the human species does not have that form of limitation. Were mankind a variety of higher ape, our species' population-potential would be in the order of the higher apes, perhaps a few millions living individuals at any one time during the recent one to two millions of years. The existence of more than six billions living human individuals today, that on a higher level per capita than ancient or medieval times, or even recent centuries, expresses a power of the human species which is absent among the beasts.

That notion of power is associated with the use of the term *dynamis* by Pythagoreans and Platonists of the ancient Classical Greek culture of which European civilization's best achievements have been an outgrowth since. In ancient, pre-Euclidean Classical Greek instances, *dynamis* is a principle of *physical geometry,* not today's usually taught classroom geometry. The pre-Sophist, anti-Euclidean notion of physical geometry rejected any attempt, such as that of the Sophist Euclid, to treat geometric forms of existence as "self-evident." The doubling of the cube by construction, by the Pythagorean Archytas, the construction of the series of Platonic solids by the circles of Plato, and the later discoveries of the *Pentagramma Mirificum* by Napier and then Gauss, are examples of the way in which the Classical Greek scientific tradition defined universal physical principles in terms of construction within the medium of *a synthetic, physical geometry,* as Bernhard Riemann defined a modern form of such a physical geometry.

The measure of performance of a physical economy is the increase of the power, in that sense, of the society's population. This increase is associated with the effects of discovery and application of both universal physical principles respecting man's action on nature, and the development of Classical artistic principles of composition through which the willful social action within society is able to shape higher qualities of cooperation in society, as by development of natural law.

The measure of the performance of an economy lies within the economy of a certain population and territory as a whole, not an aggregate of the apparent gains in merely some part of the economic system. Thus, whereas digital systems can measure certain among the shadows of an intrinsically non-linear action, they can not measure the actual action itself.

Therefore, any competent science of economy must be a science of physical economy, rather than a monetary system.

What monetary systems have done, from the known surviving archeological evidence of ancient Mesopotamia on to today, is to assume that simple linear aggregations of things are the characteristic of cultures. So, modern Venetian and related doctrines assume, as Adam Smith and his predecessors did, that there are mysterious beings acting from under the floor-boards of the universe, beings casting crooked dice to determine which dwellers above shall be enriched and which impoverished, which shall be master, and which shall be slave.

Since all universal physical principles are expressed in mathematics as the efficient action of infinitesimals, as I shall emphasize below, no linear system, such as taught accounting doctrines, can actually account for the role of "investment" in discovery and use of the physical principles upon which depends any actual improvement in an economy, per capita and per square kilometer.

The relevant feature of the modern computer is, on principle, as old as humanity's earliest explorations of the subjects of astronomy, especially the development of a scientific method of astronavigation corresponding to the Egyptian notion of *Sphaerics* adopted by the Pythagoreans and Plato. However, historically, the modern idea of constructing a general-purpose machine to assist in making relevant calculations, is focussed around the implications of two qualitatively distinct sets of discoveries, the discovery of universal gravitation, as this occurred, uniquely, in the work of Johannes Kepler, and the correlation of the implications of Kepler's own discovery with the defining of the principle of "quickest pathway" by Fermat.

However, on a deeper level in the history of European civilization, the notion of such kinds of principles expressed in the form of those two discoveries, was already grasped in European civilization no later than the work, on the subject of what was identified as *Sphaerics*, by the Pythagoreans and Plato. The use of the physical principle of the catenary, by F. Brunelleschi, to construct the cupola of the Cathedral of Florence, and the articulation of the method of modern experimental physical science by Nicholas of Cusa, formed the basis for the relevant work of avowed Cusa followers such as Luca Pacioli and Leonardo da Vinci.

Although the relevant concept of principle was set forth by Cusa, the crucial step toward the practice of modern physical science, and toward the development of the modern general purpose computer, was the work of avowed Cusa follower Johannes Kepler.

With those qualifications taken into account, Kepler (not Copernicus, and certainly not that charlatan and house-lackey of Venice's Paolo Sarpi, Galileo) was the founder of the general practice of the modern experimental physical science prescribed, as to principles, by the Nicholas of Cusa who already echoed the discovery of Aristarchus of Samos made long before Copernicus. It is to be understood, respecting the origins of the computer, that the first known step toward crafting a general purpose computer was made by Kepler, to aid him in processing the vast mass of calculations through which he ridiculed the fraudulent constructions of the Roman hoaxster Claudius Ptolemy, and corrected the systemic errors in method and conception of both Copernicus and Kepler's own immediate predecessor Tycho Brahe. These specific distinctions are of crucial importance for their relevance to any competent understanding of the role of modern physical science in economy, and are also crucial for sorting myth from reality in the role of modern computing machinery developed since Kepler's contribution.

Kepler's discoveries involve a massive mathematical labor, starting with the uncompleted work of Tycho Brahe, and proceeding to correct important errors in Brahe's work, while, at the same time, completely redefining the experimental design of the system of the observations made by Brahe and others earlier.[6] Until recently, with relatively rare exceptions, most of this work of Kepler remained unknown to modern physicists generally, most notably among English-speaking populations victimized by the cults of Galileo and Newton; whereas, a bowdlerized misrepresentation of

---

6. The discovery of a heliocentric orbit had been made by Aristarchus of Samos. Kepler's discovery was of a principle of heliocentric gravitation for the Solar System as a whole.

the discoveries, as promoted by the sophist Galileo Galilei, prevailed among the devotees of Isaac Newton and their followers. That ignorance of essential features of Kepler's work, an ignorance promoted in attempted defense of the relatively popularized, synthetic image of the person of Isaac Newton, has done great damage to understanding of even the rudimentary aspects of a competent modern physical science in general, and a physical science of economy particularly. As the case of Kepler's elliptical orbit attests, the most crucial issues are elementary ones.

However, it must be noted, that the usual fallacy encountered in treatments of Kepler's and related work today, is the evasion of the issue of the efficiency of universal physical principles, such as gravitation, by substituting the mere algebraic form of representation of an apparent effect, for the actually efficient principle itself. In the extreme expression of that error of reductionist method, the idea of the physical principle as such is eliminated, by putting a mere mathematical formula in place of the notion of an efficient principle.

To present and resolve the leading issues which a sane understanding of the abilities and limitations of the digital computer demands, it is most useful to compare the principle of gravitation, as Kepler actually discovered it, with the fundamental principle of a competent physical science of economy. In other words, we must recognize the inherent, physically principled limitations of the modern general-purpose computer, and also the functional principle of successful physical economy, as expressed in the ontologically actual (not imaginary) form of the Leibnizian infinitesimal, as Leibniz's uniquely original discovery of the infinitesimal calculus directly echoed Kepler's discovery of the infinitesimal as the characteristic functional feature of the planetary orbit.

Computer Animations

This distinction which I have just made above, is the key to an invaluable quality of practice which I have introduced into our association's economics practice.

During the 1950s, as part of my professional work as a consultant in economics matters, I had seen it to be necessary to bring the notion of *dynamics*, in Leibniz's sense of the term, into ordinary economics practice. My view of the subject of dynamic economic models, as opposed to mechanistic, linear ones, can be compared with the use of the concept of *dynamics* by V.I. Vernadsky, for defining the special chemistry of the Bio-

sphere, as I have emphasized that in my 2005 "Vernadsky and Dirichlet's Principle."

The principle is the same employed for music, as by the conductor Wilhelm Furtwängler's notion of "performing between the notes." The principle of the Pythagorean *comma*, as applied to the method of well-tempered counterpoint of J.S. Bach, is the relevant consideration. In all cases, economy, biogeochemistry, and Classical polyphony, we are dealing with phenomena which have the quality of an anti-Euclidean physical geometry. This is the same principle established for modern physical science generally by Bernhard Riemann's founding, and development of an explicitly anti-Euclidean geometry. This is a physical geometry from which all *a priori* assumptions of definitions, axioms, and postulates are banned, in which only experimentally established universal physical principles exist for science, as also for Classical artistic composition and related practice.

In such anti-Euclidean systems, as outlined by Riemann beginning with his 1854 habilitation dissertation, the only "dimensions" permitted are universal physical-experimental principles. On this account, Riemann's habilitation dissertation represents a return to the implicit core-principle of the method of *Sphaerics* employed by the Pythagoreans and Plato. In physical economy (which is to say real economy, as distinct from a mere monetary-financial system), it is the gain in what Norbert Wiener misnamed "negative entropy" which is of essential relevance.

For example, my work of 1948-1953, which carried me to the point of successfully defining a physical-economic function in economy as a Riemannian function, prescribed that economic processes must be defined implicitly as physical-economic processes, such that performance of monetary-financial systems must be judged, as I have written here earlier, from the standpoint of a physical, non-monetary process. This means treating all relevant physical principles of human activity as a process which is to be assessed for its relative, physical "anti-entropy." This means, that the development of the universe to a higher state of organization, as the case of the emergence of the Solar System from the Sun illustrates the point, is expressed in the form of mankind's discovery and expression of additional universal physical principles. This implicitly defines the physical significance of a Riemannian species of hyper-geometrical notion of dynamics.

In the simplest practical application of this outlook

on the U.S. economy, considering evidence over a lapse of time such as the recent sixty years, we use the annual changes in the physical statistical characteristics of the U.S. political county, as the convenient political-economic unit of approximation required for today's analytical work. We then compare changes in physical-economic parameters, so, county by county, over a span of decades. We take into account an increasing number of physical factors. In this process, our attention must be principally focussed on two kinds of phenomena portrayed by using this approach. We are contrasting linear patterns with significantly non-linear patterns. We must be chiefly concerned with significant non-linear effects of a sort we might otherwise associate with such matters as "changes in quality of life" experienced in counties.

The study divides the county's physical-economic processes between what may be best classed as the working distinction between "basic economic infrastructure" and direct production, the latter as by private enterprises. Power, water, public transportation, health-care facilities, schools and related, and so on are featured as "infrastructure." Agriculture, manufacturing, and privately supplied technical services not included under "infrastructure," compose the second principled category.

The relatively greatest importance is attributed to those characteristically non-linear changes in patterns associated with addition, improvement, or loss, or deterioration in categories of elements of infrastructure and the private sector. Typical, in the 1968-2006 interval, is the often catastrophic degree of entropic collapse of county economies caused by loss of technologically progressive family farming (as distinct from large-scale corporate farming), and by replacement of skilled, capital-intensive employment by low-skilled forms of non-capital-intensive, so-called "services employment."

The most significant categories within such studies are relative capital-intensity, level of scientific technology, relative "energy-flux density," and addition or removal of specific forms of technology from production or infrastructure, either by elimination, or merely by technological or other forms of attrition. These are the typical correlatives of manifest "non-linear" discontinuities in the observed function. The sharpest manifestations are associated with the introduction of a newly adopted physical principle for practice, or a loss of the participation of such a principle which would probably result in a discontinuous form of collapse within the local economy.

In reviewing such developments over the 1945-2006 interval to date, we must recognize that the phenomenon of the Sixty-Eighters represented the coming to adulthood of the relevant portion of the sociologically upper twenty-percentile of the "Baby Boomer" generation born between, approximately, 1945-1957. The hard-core "Sixty-Eighters'" countercultural trend of hatred against technological progress in economy, against so-called "blue-collar workers" and progressive family farming, represented a shift in cultural impulse, away from the science-driver trends in the economy under President Franklin Roosevelt, as continued, with approximate consistency, through the assassination of President John F. Kennedy, toward what Zbigniew Brzezinski hailed as a radically entropic form of "technetronic" cultural change, the change carried through by the successive Nixon and Carter Administrations.

That was the predecessor for the more violent destruction of the world economy led by the Synarchist financier circles associated with André Meyer's protégé Felix Rohatyn, whose proposed pro-globalization policies would reduce the sustainable population of the planet, from the present level of more than six billions, to about the levels which the planet "enjoyed" during the period of Europe's mid-Fourteenth-Century "New Dark Age."

Thus, what we are measuring in reviewing the physical-economic realities of the post-1968 U.S.A. is an accelerating entropy in the economy, and conditions of life of the U.S.A. as a whole.

When I refer to computer "animations," my emphasis is on showing the effects of adding, or removing one or more physical principles from the economic process represented. It is to be borne in mind, that analytically useful forms of computer animations are, conceptually, an outgrowth of the use of lapsed-time photography, especially the use of such techniques for assisting the mind of the observer in seeing the determined, "intentional" patterns of motion, as in comparison of the growth patterns of some weeds with those of other plants. I have recommended the use of computer animations generally, but I have emphasized, properly, that it is the instances of authentically "non-linear" functions, such as those associated with the addition or removal of an applied physical principle in the process represented, which is what we must prefer to discover and represent.

2. What Is 'Non-Linear,' Strictly Speaking?

Perhaps, this may seem curious, but, within the bounds of physiological limitations, opposite to digital computers, true scientists tend, within limits, to become better thinkers, if slower, as they grow older. The same is true in principle among great Classical artists, except that the waning of powers of vision and hearing tend to constrict their sensory experiences, performances, as similar problems of ageing impair the scientist's capacity for certain types of hands-on experimental work. The root cause for this apparent anomaly in human physiology, is that, as Russia's V.I. Vernadsky made clear during the closing decade of his life, the human individual belongs, as Mosaic **Genesis** 1 prescribes, to a qualitatively higher domain of existence than any form of animal life. *Man, when functioning as a human being, is mortal as animals are, and therefore subject to frailty; but, man is neither a mere machine, nor a mere animal. Human creativity is not an animal quality; whereas, human stupidity does appear to qualify as an animal quality.*

In other words, just as living processes have a chemistry which does not exist in the abiotic behavior of the same atomic elements, so analogously, the functional distinction of the human mind is absolutely set apart from the domain of animal ecology by those creative (e.g., *noëtic*) powers which are unique to the internal life of the individual human mind. The effect of these *noëtic* powers can not be communicated directly from one individual to another, as if by "wiring," but only replicated through the principle of "resonance," as typified by the role of irony in Classical poetry, or by methods such as conductor Wilhelm Furtwängler's "performing between the notes."

As Vernadsky's argument, respecting the Noösphere, implicitly requires, the human cognitive powers which are expressed by original discoveries of universal physical principles, such as Kepler's discovery of gravitation, or Archytas' doubling of the cube entirely by physical-geometric construction, are the expression of a universal physical principle, in the same sense that the chemistry of the dynamic action of living processes includes actions which do not occur among the same elements in non-living processes. We are dealing, thus, with what are to be regarded as distinct, but interactive physical phase-spaces, in that sense.

Cognitive creativity, as this distinguishes the human individual from the beast, is the expression of a specific physical principle, but it is a principle which supersedes the merely living phase-space, just as life is a universal, principled, physical phase-space, distinct from the inferior, non-living phase-space. It is the physically efficient action, on the living domain, by the higher principle expressed by human creativity of the type which the Classical Greeks knew as *dynamis,* which prompts the living tissue of the human being to perform dynamic actions in categories, which we recognize in Archytas, Plato, Kepler, et al., which do not occur in the lower species.

On the "down side," so to speak, the human mind can be trained, by the kind of misuse of its specifically creative powers which Aeschylus' Olympian Zeus demands of mortal men and women, to cause mortal human individuals to suppress those creative powers, as the fraudulent Sophistry of Euclid did with the discoveries of those physical principles of geometry which had been made earlier by such as the Pythagoreans and Plato. Such has been the tendency toward effects we encounter in philosophical reductionism, such as empiricism and pro-Machian positivism generally, as those earlier hoaxes of D'Alembert, de Moivre, Euler, Lagrange, et al., had been exposed as such by Carl F. Gauss's 1799 doctoral dissertation, and the related hoaxes of Immanuel Kant's *Critiques* and the Romantic positivism in law of G.W.F. Hegel. The effect of Mach's pernicious influence on the training of the human mind, is typified by both the case of Sigmund Freud, and the savage, fraudulent attacks on Max Planck by the German-speaking followers of the Mach cult during the period of World War I. These defective personalities, such as Freud and some among the Machians, did not lose those human powers, as Freud, for example, had brilliant moments; rather, those powers were largely suppressed, and, in that process, the creative potential was often expressed in the form of a reductionist perversion.

The fact that our universe is composed of three distinct, but interacting sets of principles, is, in itself, the basis for an ontological proof, that the interrelationship among the three categories of principle, shows the existence of a higher principle, a higher, subsuming, "fourth domain," under which the three respectively distinct phase-spaces are integrated into a single dynamic system.

\ *John von Neumann with his ENIAC computer. Von Neumann's superstitious notions of "artificial intelligence," along with the Cybernetics project of Norbert Wiener et al., "has been the crucial ideological feature of the method by which the once mighty U.S. economy, among others, has systematically destroyed itself over the course of the 1968-2006 period to date."*

For those reasons, the reasons illustrated by Plato in his **Parmenides** dialogue, the fruit of these creative powers can not be communicated within the bounds of an arithmetic, nor of a Euclidean geometry. In the matter of creativity, all deductive-inductive method fails absolutely.

Thus, the human individual has a quality of potential immortality which is not available to any lower form of living process. As Nicholas of Cusa emphasized, animals, at their best, may achieve implied immortality only through their participation in an absolutely, distinctly higher form of existence, mankind, as man's immortality is located in participation in a higher domain, the "fourth domain," the universe of the Creator.

The contrary views, such as the Sophist view adopted by Euclid's **Elements**, defines an essentially linear, flat-Earth universality of the parallel postulate. Substituting a non-Euclidean postulate for the parallel postulate, improves the appearance, but does not bring the dead back to life. Remove the arbitrary assumptions of Euclidean or other implicitly "flat-Earth" geometries, and nothing is left for science but a dynamic system, a finite and self-bounded universe which is im-

plicitly a Riemannian form of hypergeometry.

That situates the following parameters for treatment of the subject of the radically positivist rant of Russell, Wiener, von Neumann, et al.

To sum up the argument with which I have introduced this chapter of my report: the effect of this qualitative distinction of mankind from beasts, is demonstrated in a manner which coincides with Vernadsky's conception of the qualitative, universal distinction of three qualities of perceptible existence in the universe: the non-living processes, the domain of living processes known as the *Biosphere*, and the third, higher domain, the domain of mankind, which Vernadsky named as the *Noösphere*.

As Vernadsky's work in biogeochemistry shows, the barrier between the domain of the abiotic, and of the living processes and their fossils, expresses a universal physical principle. So, there is a principled barrier which sets the human individual above the beasts. Mankind is the only species which can willfully increase its potential relative population-density, per square kilometer of the Earth's total surface. This distinction is the only competent basis for defining, and assessing the quality of the practice of economy.

Thus, as I have presented the argument in my "Vernadsky and Dirichlet's Principle," Vernadsky's work done during the closing decade of his life, rounded out the proof that the physical universe, as we experience it, is divided among three categorical, but dynamically interacting domains: non-living; life and its specific products; and, the processes of cognition which set the human individual into a category in a higher, third domain, outside the domain of other living processes.

Vernadsky defined these distinctions in terms of *dynamics*, as Leibniz introduced the term "dynamics" into modern physical science. Instead of locating action within the extended, specifically Euclidean domain of

René Descartes and his British and continental empiricist followers, Vernadsky's conception of dynamics is, like Leibniz's, a faithful echo of the science of *Sphaerics* associated with the scientific discoveries of the Pythagoreans and Plato. Real universal action occurs within an *anti-Euclidean* physical geometry, as this is best typified for modern physical science by the work of Bernhard Riemann.

So, as I stated at the outset of this present chapter: those who employ their mind, more emphatically, for the kind of acts of creative insight which we associate with discoveries of universal physical principle, and the like, rather than the lower order of deductive-inductive argument, tend to strengthen their intellectual powers, in certain respects, as time passes, relative to those whose mental habits remain relatively "ossified" over time. The class of phenomena associated with this distinction, can not be traced within the bounds of biology as such, but obliges us to take into account the fact that cognitive action, such as that associated with discoveries of scientific principle, expresses a power which is of a higher order than biology, and acts thus upon it, *dynamically*.

This distinction corresponds in intention to the assignment, in **Genesis** 1, of a higher mission to man and woman. No animal species can increase its potential relative population-density, but only man, and that through means of the higher, cognitive function through which such effects as the discovery and use of higher orders of universal physical principles are generated by those non-degenerate cultures which have contempt for, and hate the satanic figure of the Olympian Zeus of Aeschylus' **Prometheus Bound**.

This dynamic quality of mind is typical of the best known among ancient Classical Greeks, such as Thales, Heraclitus, Solon, Archytas, Socrates, and Plato, but lacking in their notable adversaries. The proper use of the term "dynamic," as employed by Leibniz in opposition to Descartes and Descartes' followers, is a modern expression derived from the intention of the Classical Greek Pythagoreans' use of "*dynamis*," and has a modern ontological connotation corresponding to the Classical Greek usage of Plato et al. respecting the application of the notion of an efficiently physical, rather than a merely formal geometry.

For convenience at this point, let us describe the significance of that use of the term "dynamics," as it appears in contrast to the radically reductionist systems of modern empiricist and positivist ideologies. In this way, we shall provide the reader an intellectual map of the topics to be discussed in the following pages.

Kepler's Self-Bounded Universe

The universe of Riemann and Einstein, for example, is a *dynamic* system, of a type best described, as I have above, as *finite and self-bounded*. That means, for example, that gravity, as discovered uniquely by Johannes Kepler (but not the modern sophists Galileo and Newton) is *an efficiently universal physical principle*. This means, in other words, a principle of action as extensive as the universe, in a universe which extends no further than is reached by the universal principle of gravitation. Our universe is therefore self-bounded, and finite in that sense. Its bounds are expressed in mankind's expanding accumulation of discoveries and applications of universal physical principles.

Therefore, as I have said, each discovery which meets the requirements of a universal physical principle, is also as extensive and bounded as gravitation is to be defined as bounded. The principles which satisfy that requirement, interact universally, to produce those commonly bounded effects which are discovered in the course of mankind's expanding knowledge of experience.

Therefore, all physical action in the universe is defined by a physical geometry which expresses the universal interaction of universal physical principles. The universe is, therefore, pervasively *dynamic* in these terms. It is the adducibly distinct categories of dynamics which define the distinction of the otherwise interactive abiotic, Biosphere, and Noösphere. The interaction among these three domains defines the experimental domain of the known universe as a unified set of phase-spaces as a whole.

The issue of human practice so posed, thus assumes the form of: *How does man, through aid of his sense-apparatus, know, with certainty, of the existence of any universal physical principle?* For modern physical science's practice, Johannes Kepler's discovery of universal gravitation, presents what appears to me now, to be the best choice of illustration of the notion of a universal physical principle as an intrinsically non-linear, or *transcendental* function of the type which required the development of not only Gottfried Leibniz's own, uniquely original discovery of the infinitesimal calculus, but the addition of the revolutionary change in mathematical physics carried out by Bernhard Riemann's development of an absolutely anti-Euclidean physical geometry.

The leading accomplishment of Riemann for physical science in general, was to go beyond the limits of elliptical functions, including the limits of Abel's work, to explore and develop deeper implications of Gauss's passing attention to the subject of hypergeometries. (By which I mean to reject the attempt to inflict Riemann with support for a discovery which the caught-out plagiarist and hoaxster Cauchy had copied from a paper he had stolen from the writings of the deceased Abel. The stolen paper turned up, at Cauchy's death, in a cataloguing of the materials carefully filed among Cauchy's possessions.)

Consider the principle of gravity in this way, a discovery made uniquely by Johannes Kepler. I use this case here to illustrate the quality of intention which should underlie the use of animation in treating the subject of physical economy.

The *mistaken description* of Kepler's discovery would be to say, that the planet, such as Earth or Mars, follows an elliptical pathway within the Solar System. The *competent choice of scientific language,* says, that universal principle known as gravity, repeatedly compels the planet to follow what becomes an elliptical pathway. The principled character of that action which might be portrayed at the blackboard of mere Euclidean geometry, as by pins and strings, or by an appropriate cross-sectional cut of a cone, expresses methods which have nothing in common with the ontological character of an elliptical Keplerian orbit. The crude options are typical of the usually miseducated student, as among the followers of Descartes and Newton. The correct method defines the need for a Leibnizian development of an ontologically infinitesimal calculus.

It was a conception consistent with the latter, appropriate choice of language, which impelled Kepler to present two challenges to the future mathematicians who might continue to perfect his own original discovery. This conception by Kepler, as addressed successfully by Leibniz, Carl Gauss, and others, through the work of Bernhard Riemann, is the key for understanding the proper function which animations should perform in study of the lawful principles governing the patterns of behavior of the U.S. and all other economies—whether the government, or governments, agree to this, or not.

The two challenges delivered by Kepler were, first,

to develop *a truly infinitesimal calculus,* and, second, to define, not a mere mathematics as such, but a mathematical physics of *elliptical functions,* the latter premised on the crucial experimental evidence of Kepler's work: that it was the gravitation which generated the *ontologically infinitesimal* form of action corresponding to an ellipse. All competent mathematical physics must be proven within the bounds of those two, interdependent aspects of Kepler's own original discovery. These same two considerations are also, approximately, the foundation of a competent science of physical economy.

On the first count, the vector which impels the planet along the generated orbital pathway, changes in each instant, no matter how small the estimated lapse of time during that instant. In other words, contrary to the empiricist Newtonians such as Euler, Lagrange, Cauchy, et al., the orbit is, *ontologically, absolutely infinitesimal.* The action which this infinitesimal expresses is, in actuality, not imaginary, as de Moivre, D'Alembert, Euler, et al., insisted; it expresses the efficiently acting presence of the universality of the principle expressed, for example, as gravitation. On this account, Kepler assigned the task of creating a calculus of the infinitesimal to future mathematicians.

To restate the core of that argument: gravitation is not a matter of an interaction (as if at a distance) among discrete bodies, but a pervasive action by a universal existence upon the universe in which any body is situated, *dynamically*, at any time. All universal principles have that same efficient character expressed in their effects.

Within the bounds of European civilization since the ancient Greece of Thales and Solon of Athens, this fact about universal physical principles would tend to be grasped more or less readily, as it was by the Pythagoreans and Plato. The impediment to clear thinking has been the type of reductionist Sophistry typified, for geometry, by Euclid's **Elements**. The reductionists' assumption that action occurs among discrete bodies within a predetermined, linear ordering of a purely formal physical space-time, is the induced quality of insanity which continues to be the leading obstacle to sanity respecting matters of science to the present time.

Rather than accepting the fact that sense-perception is the shadow which the real universe tends to cast upon our sense-organs, and, then, seeking to discover the experimental principles which show us *the process of generation of a real universe beyond the shadows,* the reductionist interprets sense-perception—the shadows cast upon the senses by reality—as reality per se. The pathetic effect of the reductionist assumption is, in effect, something akin to the notion that definitions, axioms, and postulates are self-evidently existing agencies of cause and effect. Thus, Riemann's bold return to the standpoint of *Sphaerics*, in his 1854 habilitation dissertation and beyond, is the necessary modern correction for the pathetic influences of reductionism in general and the standpoints of Descartes and Newton in particular.

The Leibniz calculus, from its initial development, no later than 1676 Paris, to its later precision as a catenary/natural-logarithmic-cued universal principle of physical least-action, meets Kepler's requirement. The reductionist counterfeits, such as that attributed to Isaac Newton, and to the doctrines of the empiricists D'Alembert, de Moivre, Euler, Lagrange, Laplace, and Cauchy, do not meet the requirement.

On the second count, it was clear to Kepler that we must not situate any physical principle, such as gravitation, within an aprioristic, Euclidean or kindred sort of Sophist system. The principle of hypergeometry since Riemann, has been, that the curvature lies within *the dynamic nature* of the action, rather than the action within the curvature. The three most outstanding cases of those who mastered Kepler's challenge on this account, were Carl F. Gauss, Niels Abel, and Bernhard Riemann. Riemann adopted Gauss's treatment of both elliptical physical functions and the rudiments of the higher-order physical-hypergeometric functions, as starting-points for what emerged as the Riemannian physical geometry which underlies any competent modern approach to a science of physical economy.

On this account, it should be emphasized that Kepler's method, which he rightly bases on the influence of Nicholas of Cusa and Leonardo da Vinci, is already, implicitly, a method of physical geometry, not an "ivory tower" mathematics such as that of Euclid. The outcome of the successive discoveries of Leibniz, Gauss, Riemann, et al., is already implicit in the work of Kepler. This was already recognized as a matter of *a threatening principle, contrary to their special interests*, by the empiricist followers of the New Venetian Party of Paolo Sarpi, as the attempt to destroy knowledge of Kepler's work was deployed through hoaxsters such as Fludd, Sarpi's lackey Galileo, Descartes, and the Isaac Newton hoax steered by Abbé Antonio Conti, et al. Once again, in this and comparable cases, the voice of the Satanic Olympian Zeus, heard in Aeschy-

lus' ***Prometheus Bound***, resonates in the misty unwashed nooks of the modern science classroom.

The type of creative conceptions which I have defended here, conceptions situated within the domain of an epistemologically competent modern science, were not original to modern Europe; they are rooted in the earlier scientific practice of *Sphaerics*, which the ancient Classical Greek Pythagoreans and Plato adopted from Egyptian origins. Knowledge of that connection is more than probably indispensable in today's world, to clear up the popularized, false assumptions which were embedded in the wicked tradition of ancient Sophists such as the famous Euclid.

How Sophistry Corrupts Science

My experience with my own original discoveries in the science of physical economy, combined with experience of the achievements and shortcomings within the that the proper approach to the development of a new adult generation of more fruitfully creative minds is to concentrate on avoiding the replication of those traditional pedagogical hoaxes of the classroom. The experience of a lifetime has shown me, that a young mind which submits to qualifying himself, or herself in a profession by submitting to the canons of a corrupt representation of science, is more likely to damage his, or her mind, than improve it.

By premising the education of bright young adult minds on avoiding the pitfalls called the taught canons of science and modern art, we leave young adult minds of promise free to unleash their true potential. Given the circumstances under which progress has proceeded, the work of the LYM during the recent several years on this account, has been a gratifying success in the specific sense that it shows the pathway to travel in promoting the creative development of the individual mind.

Cardinal Nicholas of Cusa appears thus as the most notable among the great creative intellects who shaped the wonderful work of the great "Golden Renaissance" of the mid-Fifteenth Century. From the vantage-point of the contemporary classroom, ***De Docta Ignorantia*** seems an awkward work, as all great beginnings of a valid intellectual revolution must be. It appears difficult in its own way, because every work of pioneering a new quality of direction in the Classical modes of science and art, must create its own language as it proceeds from the beginnings of a new direction. If later works appear less awkward, it is chiefly because the richer development of the necessary forms of language, and of ideas as such, have enriched the catalogue of our conversations. Such is the way in which real creativity proceeds, especially those creative efforts which launch an entire field of scientific or comparable thought.

The great accomplishments within modern European culture, although they echo, chiefly, the Classical Greek legacy established prior to the Roman, Byzantine, and medieval systems of corruption, were brought forth afresh by the Renaissance and its immediate predecessors, giving newly minted names for ideas almost lost to historical memory, and introducing new ideas not known to predecessors. In the greatest of the art and science which has emerged in the aftermath of the Fifteenth-Century Renaissance of Cusa et al., we have accumulated a new language, not merely of new words, but of new conceptions of principle unknown to our civilization's predecessors. As the participants in the experience of the LYM's self-development turn to Classical science and music, they find available to them a rich vocabulary of selectable, non-linear ideas of science and Classical art which have been created by six centuries of progress—despite the reactionary setbacks along the way. Ideas which had been confined to awkward expression, now have a rich vocabulary on which to improve.

The attempted corruption of ancient Greek science did not begin with Euclid. The intersecting, combined influence of the reductionists, such as the "materialists," Aristotle, and Euclid, have been the principal reservoirs of such types of intellectual corruption in European civilization since, up into modern times. The kernel of that corruption can be fairly summarized, for our purposes here, in the following way.

As I have already stressed this point above: we know that our imagination of what we are experiencing in the world, so to speak, which is "outside our skins," is not necessarily a competent representation of the real world. What our consciousness experiences is our attempt to discover both how the universe in which we live is controlled, and how we might alter the way in which that control is exerted.

Do not ignore sign-posts, but, at the same time, never allow yourselves to be duped into believing in mere signs, such as mere mathematical formulations.

FIDELIO

Journal of Poetry, Science, and Statecraft

From the first issue, dated Winter 1992, featuring Lyndon LaRouche on "The Science of Music: The Solution to Plato's Paradox of 'The One and the Many,'" to the final issue of Spring/Summer 2006, a "Symposium on Edgar Allan Poe and the Spirit of the American Revolution," *Fidelio* magazine gave voice to the Schiller Institute's intention to create a new Golden Renaissance.

The title of the magazine, is taken from Beethoven's great opera, which celebrates the struggle for political freedom over tyranny. *Fidelio* was founded at the time that LaRouche and several of his close associates were unjustly imprisoned, as was the opera's Florestan, whose character was based on the American Revolutionary hero, the French General, Marquis de Lafayette.

Each issue of *Fidelio*, throughout its 14-year lifespan, remained faithful to its initial commitment, and offered original writings by LaRouche and his associates, on matters of, what the poet Percy Byssche Shelley identified as, "profound and impassioned conceptions respecting man and nature."

Back issues are now available for purchase through the Schiller Institute website:
http://schillerinstitute.org/about/order_form.html